The Limerick Makers

A fig for the growls of the grumbler!

John O'Toumy

Published by THE BORROWDALE PRESS 2000
17 Dixon Road Norwich NR7 8QJ
Telephone: +44(0)1603 419411

First published by The Research Publishing Co. in 1976
This edition published by The Borrowdale Press in 2004

DESIGN: ANGELA BARSON
PRINTED BY RICHARD CLOVER LITHO, ACLE, NORFOLK

ISBN 0–9540349–3–7

The Limerick Makers

Jean Harrowven

The Borrowdale Press 2000
Norwich

Our life is not what it seems,
It never pours, but it teems,
   But if we make cheer
   With what we have here
We need never resort to our dreams.

J.H.

As Dennis Norden says, limerick making is a talent like wiggling your ears, or drawing likenesses — which you have or you haven't got. If you have got the talent then you will enjoy reading this book. If you haven't —then read it anyway — you might acquire a new slant on the humorous side of life for —

No matter how grouchy you're feeling
You'll find the smile more or less healing;
It grows in a wreath
Around the front teeth —
Thus preserving the face from congealing.

A.Euwer

Contents

List of Illustrations

Personal Acknowledgments

I should like to record my thanks to the librarians of the following institutions:

The Osborne collection of children's books, Toronto Library; Dublin Central Library; The Royal Irish Academy; Limerick County Library; *The Daily Mail* Records Department; Society of Authors; Castle Museum, Norwich; Bridewell Museum, Norwich; Norwich Central Library; St William's Way Library, Norfolk.

Thank you —

Mannix Joyce, Jack Gowers, Trevor Bailey, Dr Robert Wyse Jackson, Dr S.C. Bulley, Miss Ida Thurtle, Miss Elsie Bennell, *The Daily Mail, The Eastern Evening News, The Limerick Leader,* BBC1 *Look East*, BBC Forwarding Service, the children and staff of Thorpe St Andrew School, Norfolk.

All well known personalities who have so sportingly contributed — and many others without whose verses this book would not have been possible.

JEAN Harrowven, a Froebel trained teacher gave up her career to concentrate on writing. She specialises in historical research both for the adult and children's markets. She also writes humorous books for children.

The Limerick Makers is the result of much thought and research by the author, and she feels that the mystery of the origin of the limerick verse has at last been solved.

The book traces the development and use of this popular verse form, from the first Gaelic limericks sung in the mid-eighteenth to the late twentieth century. It gives refreshing biographies of Edward Lear and Herbert Langford Reed who were great limerick men. The last chapter is composed of limericks sent to the author by comedians and artistes known and remembered by the general public.

In fact the book is well illustrated throughout with examples written by 'limerick makers' from all over the English speaking world.

Jean Harrowven lives with her husband and daughter in a quiet hamlet just outside Norwich. Her son lives in Kent. Her hobbies range from writing books, playing bridge and gardening.

INTRODUCTION

THIS is not an anthology. Indeed, a straight collection of limericks would be boring. The restrictive nature of the metre lends itself to monotony, and therefore limericks are acceptable only in small doses.

This type of verse is not acclaimed as poetry by the literary world, and in many anthologies of humorous verse it is ignored altogether. There is no scope for deep expression within its walls. Also, as William Cole points out in his *Fireside Book of Humorous Poetry* —

The limerick packs laughs anatomical,
Into space that is quite economical;
But the good ones I've seen
So seldom are clean,
And the clean ones so seldom are comical!

I do not entirely agree with this idea, as I have come across many that are comical *and* clean, but of course the provocative form does lend itself to unprintable versions.

The critics say, and rightly so, that the British public's taste for poetry is very low, and the limerick may be considered to be the only verse form known and liked by the majority. It is easy to compose, dashing, and contains something indefinable in the metre that ignites humour. The layman is drawn to it — has a stab at it, and is pleased by it.

A limerick can be defined as a humorous word picture — an amusing anecdote painted with the minimum number of rhyming words. A 'maker' is an old term for a poet, and in this sense any one of us can be a limerick poet.

Up to now the historians relate that the origins of this verse form cannot be traced. In *The Oxford Dictionary of Nursery Rhymes*, p. 407, Mr and Mrs Opie write: "When the term 'limerick' first came to be applied to this type of verse, and where it comes from, is obscure."

By its very nature the limerick does not lend itself to mystery. It may be described as bold, comical, crude, but never mysterious. And yet for over 150 years its origin has baffled thinkers. And perhaps because of its trivial nature work in this direction has been spasmodic and scarce.

Most mysteries have a surprise in the last chapter, but it is always advisable to begin at the beginning, so it is in the opening chapters that I present evidence which will establish, I hope, the true birthplace of this well loved type of verse.

I include a chapter of modern children's limericks, and another on the popularity of competitions. In the section entitled 'The Entertainers' I present a collection of original and favourite limericks sent to me personally, by many well known artistes and comedians.

In fact, the purpose of this book is to trace without bias the seed and growth of the limerick — not only as a literary verse form, but as a creative urge in the minds of ordinary folk.

1
Fragments

There are surprising numbers of isolated verses written with the metrical swing of the limerick to be found in the ancient literature of many countries of the world. The easily defined metre can be found in Greek, Latin, English, French and old Gaelic manuscripts, to name a few.

In England there is evidence of this verse form, spasmodically used throughout the centuries.

We have our own *Hickory Dickory Dock*. As a nursery rhyme it was first recorded in 1744, but is known to have existed in the oral tradition long before this. A clue to its age may be gleaned when we realise that it contains relics of old numerals — probably Saxon, in the first and last lines.

Another isolated verse can be found in the British Museum's Harleian Manuscript 7322, and dates back to the fourteenth century. It is mentioned in *The Making of Verse* by Swann and Sidgwick —

The lion is wonderly strong
And full of the wiles of wo;
And whether he pleye,
Or take his preye,
He cannot do but to slo. [slay]

Swann and Sidgwick go on to define a limerick as a triple time version of the short metre — i.e. first two lines of three feet each, then a line of four feet, divided into two, followed by another line of three feet. I think this just about sums it up!

In *Othello, Hamlet* and *The Tempest* — all works by William Shakespeare, the limerick metre shows itself in isolated verses.

Ben Johnson takes up the pattern in his *Masque of the Gypsies Metamorphos'd* — entitled 'The Faery Became upon You' —

Her Eyes and Glow-worme lend thee,
The Shooting Starres attend thee;
The elves also,
Whose little eyes glow,
Like the sparke of fire befriend thee...

A piece called 'Mondayes Work' published in *The Roxburghe Ballads*, in 1640, also has the form —

Good morrow neighbour Gamble,
Come let you and I goe ramble;
Last night I was shot
Through the braines with a
pot —
And now my stomach doth wamble.

The French can produce at least two old rhymes using the limerick metre — first the equivalent of *Hickory Dickory Dock* — thought to be even older than the English version.

Digerie, digerie, doge,
Le souris ascend l'horloge;
L'horloge frappe
Le souris s'échappe,
Digerie, digerie, doge.

This rhyme was mentioned in *Boswell's Life of Johnson* —

On s'étonne ici que Caliste
Ait pris l'habit de Moliniste
Puisque cette jeunne beauté
Ote à chacun sa liberté
N'est ce pas une Janeniste?

It was written in the beginning of the eighteenth century and roughly translated it tells of a young lady who went to a masquerade ball dressed as a Jesuit, and her critics said that if she went anywhere dressed as what she was not, then in fact she was improperly dressed.

There is a surprising regular limerick beat to this old Latin prayer which dates back to the thirteenth century.

Sit vitiorum meorum evacuatio
Concupiscentiae et libidinis exterminatio,
Caritatis et patientiae,
Humilitatis et obedientiae,
Omniumque virtutum augmentatio.

It is the prayer of St Thomas Aquinas (1225-1274) and it is included in the Roman breviary of the Catholic priests throughout the world, as one of the thanksgiving prayers after Mass.

Ireland can boast a wealth of ancient literature dating back to very early times. There are many pockets of verse using the limerick metre.

'Ronan's Lament' has at least one stanza using this form. This dates back to the eighth century, and was rewritten in the eleventh.

Ro gab Echaid óinieni,
iar mbeith i leinn lebrairthe
  In brónánifil,
  for DúnnAis,
atá for Dún Sebaurche.

Mr. Doyle, the Limerick librarian, read this out to me slowly, and I could clearly define the metre, which has an internal rhyme scheme.

'Ronan's Lament' can be seen in *A Golden Treasury of Irish Poetry A.D. 600 to 1200*, edited with translations by David Greene and Frank O'Connor.

In *Best Irish Limericks* compiled by Tony Butler, the author put forward another example, taken from 'The Song of the Sea', by Rumann MacColmain, written in the eighth century, also. Here is a rough translation of one stanza —

When the wind comes from the south,
Over the shield-bearing Saxons stout,
  It drives waves up Skiddy,
  Makes high Calad Mit giddy,
Pounding the grey-green of Shannon's mouth.

This was originally edited from Kuno Meyer old manuscripts and published in vol. 2 of *Otia Merseinna*.

From the examples shown we can safely assume that the well known *33223* metre was known to scholars of many lands from early times.

But the point is — which country originally took up and developed the metre? Who were the first people to establish this verse pattern as a definite and recognised form?

I think these questions are answered convincingly, in the next chapter.

2

THE MERRY POETS OF CROOM

Once upon a time there lived a group of eleven poets and men of culture, in and around the small village of Croom, County Limerick, Ireland.

These fun-loving men were soon to be known as the Maigue Poets (Filí na Máighe). They were passionately fond of their native country, and dedicated their works to the propagation of the Irish language, which they felt was in danger of dying out, owing to the strong infiltration of English literature around the mid-eighteenth century. They were also very proud of their particular part of Ireland. The Maigue river, swift flowing through Croom, and the beautiful countryside around are immortalised in many of their poems.

The group consisted of priests, schoolmasters, men of letters, and some were self-taught. But all had the same carefree outlook on life. One poet, Séan Clárach Macdomhnaill, was held in great esteem, and regarded as the greatest Irish bard of all time.

Another was Father Nicholas O'Donnell, who was ordained at Louvain, Belgium. When he returned to Ireland he was not allowed to practise his creed, owing to the Penal Laws, but was appointed Guardian to the broken monastery of Adare. His poems were of great quality, and some have been preserved.

The two principal poets were John O'Toumy (Séan Ó Tuama),who at one time kept an inn at Croom, and his close friend Andrew McCrath (Aindrias MacCraith), who was known as 'An Mangaire Súgach' which means 'the merry pedlar'. This was because as a stranger, Andrew had bought a piece of frieze at Croom fair, and had gone around the fair with the cloth under his arm, being mistaken for a pedlar.

Later, he entered O'Toumy's pub to quaff his thirst. He eventually had too much to drink, and fell asleep after closing time. O'Toumy kindly put the young man to bed, and asked for no payment. Next morning he poured a jug of whiskey on Andrew's head and christened him 'The Merry Pedlar.'

This incident brought together two men in life-long friendship, and surely must have played an important part in establishing the true source of the limerick verse, as we know it today.

Andrew McCrath, a man with a good brain and a quick wit, decided to stay in Croom and join the Merry Poets. Like O'Toumy he sometimes did a little school-mastering in the winter, when the children were not needed to labour on the land. But, like most bards, he was generally unemployed. The poets did not care for monetary gain, and their compositions were not for sale.

O'Toumy's inn was used as a literary club, where affairs of the day were discussed, and where new pieces were sung or recited for the pleasure of the company. And, of course great quantities of liquor were consumed, which made each meeting more enjoyable than the last.

O'Toumy and McCrath were forever teasing. Although they were such good friends, they took a delight in singing sparring mini-songs to each other, on a sort of challenge-and-retort basis. They adopted the isolated verse form as seen in parts of ancient Irish literature, and coupled it with an old Irish folk tune called 'The Growling Old Woman'* — adding humour to give spice — and the 'swinging metre' — the limerick as we know it today, was born.

To the disgust of his wife, Muireann, John O'Toumy often supplied free ale when there was no money in the pockets of his customers. This jovial proprietor was no business man, and as his wife feared, he eventually was forced to give up his inn, through lack of funds.

Then followed an unhappy time for John. He had many jobs to help support his family and was at one time servant to a mean old woman — his principal task being to herd hens. She is immortalised in one of his poems.

In the latter years of his life O'Toumy managed to open another inn, in Limerick City itself, and the site in Mungret Street can still be seen today. It was here, too, that authors and literary men of the area met to exchange ideas, and it is thought that limericks were undoubtedly sung again. O'Toumy died in Limerick City, but was buried in his beloved Croom. His grave can still be seen today, and his life dates on the tomb are given as 1706–1775.

Andrew McCrath was heartbroken at his friend's death and wrote a beautiful elegy, which has been preserved. He lived another eighteen years, but it is said that he became morose and a changed man, after the loss of his friend. He died at a house in Emmet Street, Kilmallock, and is buried in the local cemetery, where in 1970, a monument to him was erected over his grave.

Manuscripts of the Maigue Poets, including many limericks and other more serious works, are in the Royal Irish Academy, Dublin, and a copy of some of the original Irish limericks can be seen in Croom branch library, today.

The poets lived in a society where printed books were almost unknown, and their compositions were recorded in a kind of shorthand, and in classical Irish, which can make

*Originally sung by a pedlar who was yoked to a scolding wife.

difficult reading, even for a person well versed in Irish.

Nevertheless, these five-lined verses have the definite dactylic rhyme pattern of *aabba* metre, and they use an internal rhyme scheme with the accent on the vowel sounds rather than the consonants.

It was not until some hundred years later, in about 1840, that a young politician and poet in his own right, one James Clarence Mangan, translated the works of the Maigue Poets. He had a very unhappy life, and died in great poverty in Dublin hospital at the age of forty-six. Like so many others, his work was not truly acclaimed until after his death, but now he is considered by some to be one of the great Irish poets. His poem 'Dark Rosaleen' is famous in Ireland today.

Mangan was well known for his translations from Irish to English — especially poetry, for which he had a special flair. In *The Life and Writings of James Clarence Mangan* by D. H. O'Donohue, published in Edinburgh in 1971, it is clear that Mangan devoted the last years of his life to presenting to the English speaking world the marvels of Irish literature.

Here is an excerpt from a letter written by Mangan to one of his friends, explaining how he will go about translating an Irish poem —

> *I would cast the translation in the same irregular metre as the original, only occasionally doubling the rhymes on a single line, which has a very good effect on an English ear.*

This is the way Mangan worked, and we can assume that his translations of the limericks of the Maigue countryside were produced using a similar formula. The same 'swinging metre' was preserved in the English version of the originals.

Here we have two challenge-and-retort verses in the traditional Irish as composed by O'Toumy and McCrath, and translated by Mangan:

Is duine mé dhíolas leann lá,
'S chuireas mo bhuíon chum remcáis,
Mura mbeadh duine im chuideachta dhíolfas
Mise bheas thíos leis in anthráth.

I sell the best brandy and sherry,
To make my good customers merry,
  But at times their finances
  Run short as it chances,
And then I feel very sad, very.

Níl binneas it' laoi ná it' sheandán,
Is ní milis dar linn do stranncán

Bíonn iomad de thoise,
Do ghloine gan líonadh,
Is d'uisce ná díge it bhranndan.

Both your poems and pints by your favour,
Are alike wholly wanting in flavour,
Because it's your pleasure
You give us short measure,
And your ale has a ditch-water savour.

The myth-like quality of the story of the Merry Poets of Croom is turned to reality when we scrutinise the facts. Nevertheless, it is easy to be romantic about these fun-loving men, who lived carefree lives, and only took pleasure and happiness in each other's company, and had no thought for money or power.

This, as I see it, is the limerick's birthright. It is a purely harmless jingle, based on humour, and designed to bring laughter and wit to the party. Its function in this respect has not altered since the day it was born.

Here is the rest of O'Toumy's 'Drinking Song' as translated by Mangan and sung to the tune of 'The Growling Old Woman' —

Here's brandy! Come fill up your tumbler;
Or ale, if your liking be humbler;
And while you've a shilling
Keep filling and swilling,
A fig for the growls of the grumbler!

I like when I'm quite at my leisure,
Mirth, music and all sorts of pleasure,
When Margery's bringing
The glass, I like singing,
With bards — if they drink without measure.

Libation I pour on libation,
I sing the past fame of our nation;
For valour won glory
For song and for story,
This, this is my grand recreation!

This was Andrew McCrath's reply —

O'Toumy! you boast yourself handy
At selling good ale and bright brandy,
  But the fact is your liquor
  Makes everyone sicker,
I tell you that, I, your friend Andy.

Again you effect to be witty
And your customers — more is the pity —
  Give into your folly,
  While you, when you're jolly,
Troll forth some ridiculous ditty.

Vile swash do you sell us for porter,
As you draw the cask shorter and shorter,
  Your guests then disdaining
  To think of complaining
Go tipple in some other quarter.

Very oft in your scant over-frothing,
Tin quarts we found little or nothing,
  They could very ill follow,
  The road, who could swallow
Such stuff for the inner man's clothing!

You sit gaily enough at the table
But in spite of your mirth you are able,
  To chalk down each tankard
  And if a man drank hard
On tick — oh we'd have such a Babel!

You bow to the floor's very level
When customers enter to revel,
  But if one in shy raiment
  Takes a drink without payment,
You score it against the poor old devil.

When quitting your house rather heady,
They'll get nought without more of "the ready"
  You'll leave them to stumble
  And stagger and tumble,
Into dykes, as folks will when unsteady.

Two vinters late went about killing
Men's fame by their vile Jack-and-Gilling;
  Now Toumy, I'll tell you
  I know very well you,
Would, too, sell us all for a shilling.

The Old Bards never vainly shall woo me,
But your tricks and your capers, O'Toumy,
  Have nought in them winning —
  You jest and keep grinning
But your thoughts are all guileful and gloomy!

Although these verses appear to be detrimental, the two men were in fact only joking with each other, and the words have no real sting.

The village of Croom, ten miles out of Limerick City has not changed much in two hundred years. Its winding village street houses many of the thousand strong population.

When I travelled to this village, I visited the Old Church of Ireland, in whose churchyard John O'Toumy was buried, in his daughter's grave. The place was overgrown and neglected and the tall yew trees cast gloomy shadows.

I paused for a while on the centuries-old Croom bridge which humps the Maigue river, and I realised why the Croom Poets were so passionately fond of their part of Ireland. The river was alive with eddies and currents, while as a contrast the banks and surrounding countryside were verdant and serene.

The people were friendly, rich with smiles and laughter, and there was an atmosphere of busy gaiety in the streets. The spirit of the Merry Poets lingered.

3
LINKS

IN between the end of the Maigue Poets' era and the first English limerick book published was a gap of about thirty to forty years. This period of time is fascinating to the researchers. It presents all kinds of questions and all kinds of answers. Owing to lack of evidence it gives the theorists a chance to have their say.

But let us first consider the existing facts.

The limericks of the Maigue Poets were sung in many Limerick pubs in the eighteenth century. At the time it is known that there existed a two-way traffic in literary ideas between Limerick City and London. Ned Purdom was a Limerick man, and a literary hack who travelled to London and back many times looking for fresh material.

Oliver Goldsmith immortalised him in his poem —

> Here lies poor Ned Purdom from misery freed,
> Who long was a bookseller's hack,
> He led such a damnable life in this world
> I don't think he'll wish to come back.

It was men like Purdom perhaps that brought the new metre to England. Grub Street, a quarter in London where poor authors met to exchange and pick up new ideas, was probably the place where the swinging metre of the limerick was first heard. This is what Dr Wyse Jackson, a noted scholar, and retired Bishop of Limerick, related in his talk at the bicentenary celebrations of the Maigue Poets held at Croom in 1970.

True, the Gaelic and meaning would be lost on English ears, but the distinguished *33223* beat of the limerick metre verse must have impressed those looking for fresh material.

Also we must not ignore the works of Thomas Moore, the celebrated Irish poet who wrote in English, and spent most of his life in England. He had connections with Limerick City, too, and was at one time asked to stand for parliament representing that city. He refused, much to the disappointment of the Irish people. He lived from 1779 to

1852, and produced a surprising number of poems and other works. He wrote occasionally using the limerick metre, and may have easily obtained ideas for this form from the works of the Maigue Poets.

Here is a stanza proclaiming loyalty to his native land —

We tread the land that bore us,
Her green flag glitters o'er us,
  The friends we've tried
  Are at our side,
And the foe we hate before us.

'The Time I've Lost in Wooing' was written at the beginning of the nineteenth century and was set to music and published with other poems, as songs entitled 'Melodies'. It uses a double stanza in each verse.

The time I've lost in wooing,
In watching and pursuing
  The light, that dies
  In woman's eyes,
Has been my heart's undoing.
Though wisdom oft has sort me,
I scorned the lore she brought me,
  My only books
  Were woman's looks,
And folly's all they've taught me.

Her smile when Beauty granted,
I hung with gaze enchanted,
  Like him, the sprite,
  Whom maids by night
Oft meet in glen that's haunted.
Like him, too, Beauty won me,
But while her eyes were on me,
  If once their ray
  Was turned away,
O! winds could not outrun me.

And are those follies going?
And is my proud heart growing
  Too cold or wise
  For brilliant eyes
Again to set it glowing?

No, vain, alas, th' endeavour
From bonds so sweet to sever;
  Poor wisdom's chance
  Against a glance
Is now as weak as ever.

It seems reasonable to assume that only the metre was obtained from Ireland. Its development and moulding into the traditional style that we know so well must be credited to English authors. For instance, the idea of using a differing place name in the first line as in 'There was an old woman of Leeds…', published in 1820 in London, produced the first geographical limerick ever to be printed.

Did the English nursery limericks as dealt with in the next chapter burst on the scene without any warning? Was there any indication of the metre evolving from earlier works? Yes, I have found many poems pre-dating 1820 which follow a similar pattern. It is only the first four beats that differ. Most of the verses I found in Leonard de Vries' charming anthology *Flowers of Delight*. This is a collection of children's verses as published in the late half of the eighteenth century, and the beginning of the nineteenth. Here are two examples — first a poem about a blind man published by Darton and Harvey in 1797 —

Good people all, both great and small,
I'm blind and cannot see,
To my surprise, I lost my eyes,
Beneath a great oak tree.

The thunder dread, crack'd round my head,
And stunned me with afright;
Then quickly came the lightning's flame,
And made me dark as night.

I have a wife, pride of my life,
But she is quite in rags,
And babies two, without a shoe,
Or stocking to their legs.

Good ladies then, and gentlemen,
I'm poor as any rat,
Your purse don't shut, but kindly put,
Some money in my hat.

Another poem in story form, issued by the same publishers starts like this —

A sweet chubby fellow,
Nam'd little Tom Dellow,
His mamma to a neighbour did lend,
With caution to stop
At a greengrocer's shop,
While she went to visit a friend.

The poor little soul,
Unus'd to control,
O'er the threshold just happened to stray,
When a sly cunning dame,
Mary Magnay by name,
Entic'd the young truant away.

There are quite a few verses tracing the story, but this poem at least, had a happy ending. *The Dandies' Ball* or *High Life in the City* was a satire for adult reading and was published independently by John Marshall in 1819, and had the same metrical pattern. This work was extremely popular and was beautifully illustrated and coloured. I have seen an original copy in the Norwich Museum, and I was very impressed by the wit and nature of the book.

We must not overlook the fact that the same publisher brought out *Anecdotes and Adventures of Fifteen Gentlemen*, the second book of English limericks ever to be published, in 1822.

Here are the first three verses of 'The Dandies' Ball' —

Mr Pilblister and Betsy his sister,
Determin'd on giving a treat,
Gay Dandies they call,
To supper and ball,
At their house in Great Camomile Street.

Mr Padum delighted, for he was invited,
Began to consider his dress,
His shirt was not clean,
Not fit to be seen,
So he washed it, he could not do less.

Here's stays from the tailor,
For Mr Macnailor,
Oh Jeffrey! Lace it quite tight.
I'll hold by the post
That no time be lost,
At the ball I'll outshine all tonight.

There are thirteen more verses in the same vein.

I think it is plain that the satirical humour of the limerick that we know so well is showing itself in the last excerpt.

It took only one more year before the first perfect English limericks were evolved — a mixture of Irish metre and English style, spiced with humour from both countries.

4

Anecdotes and Adventures

The first book of English nonsense verses, as they were called was published by John Harris and Son in 1820. This was a collection of nursery rhymes entitled *The History of Sixteen Wonderful Old Women*. The author is unknown.

There are very few original copies. One is in the Osborne collection of children's books, in Toronto Library, and there is a collection in the British Museum.

These books are so fragile, that xerocopying is done very sparingly. Each verse has a coloured cartoon-like illustration and eight can be seen in *Flowers of Delight*.

I do not know of any other book that presents all sixteen histories, except the original, but here they are —

Mistress Towl

There was an old woman named Towl
Who went out to Sea with her Owl,
But the Owl was Sea-sick
And screamed for Physic;
Which sadly annoyed Mistress Towl.

Old Woman of Croydon

There was an Old Woman of Croydon,
To look young she affected the Hoyden,
And would jump and would skip,
Till she put out her hip;
Alas poor Old Woman of Croydon.

Old Woman of Bath

There was an Old Woman of Bath,
And she was as thin as a Lath,
She was brown as a berry
With a Nose like a Cherry;
This skinny Old Woman of Bath.

Old Woman of Ealing

There once was an Old Woman of Ealing,
She jump'd till her head touched the Ceiling
When 2 1 6 4,
Was announced at her door,
As a prize to th' Old Woman of Ealing.

The Old Woman of Lynn

There liv'd an Old Woman of Lynn,
Whose nose very near touch'd her chin,
You may easy suppose,
She had plenty of Beaux;
This charming Old Woman of Lynn.

Old Woman of Exeter

There dwelt an Old Woman of Exeter,
When visitors came it sore vexed her,
So fear they should eat,
She locked up the meat;
This stingy Old Woman of Exeter.

Old Woman of Harrow

There was an Old Woman of Harrow,
Who visited in a Wheel barrow,
And her servant before,
Knock'd loud at each door,
To announce the Old Woman of Harrow.

Old Woman of Gosport

There was an Old Woman of Gosport,
And she was one of the cross sort,
While she dress'd for the ball,
Her wig was too small;
Which enrag'd this Old Woman of Gosport.

Old Woman of France

There came an Old Woman of France,
Who taught grown up Children to dance,
But they were so stiff,
She sent them home in a miff,
This sprightly Old Woman of France.

Old Woman of Leith

There was an Old Woman of Leith,
Who had a sad pain in her Teeth,
  But the Blacksmith uncouth,
  Scar'd the pain from her tooth;
Which rejoic'd the Old Woman of Leith.

Old Woman of Devon

There was an Old Woman of Devon,
Who rose every morning at seven,
  For her house to provide,
  And to warm her inside;
This provident Old Woman of Devon.

Old Woman of Spain

There was an Old Woman of Spain,
To be civil went much 'gainst the grain,
  Yet she danc'd a fandango
  With General Fernando;
This whimsical Old Woman of Spain.

Old Woman of Gloster

There was an Old Woman of Gloster,
Whose parrot two guineas it cost her;
  But his tongue never ceasing
  Was vastly displeasing
To that talkative Woman of Gloster.

Old Woman of Leeds

There was an Old Woman of Leeds,
Who spent all her life in Good Deeds,
  She worked for the poor,
  Till her fingers were sore,
This pious Old Woman of Leeds.

Old Woman of Norwich

There was an Old Woman of Norwich,
Who liv'd on nothing but porridge,
  Parading the town,
  She turned cloak into gown,
That thrifty Old Woman of Norwich.

Old Woman of Surrey

There was an Old Woman of Surrey,
Who was morn noon and night, in a hurry,
Call'd her husband a Fool,
Drove her children to school;
The worrying Old Woman of Surrey.

The person who engendered these verses must have had his tongue in his cheek when he described *The Old Women* as 'wonderful'. But they did represent a down to earth cross-section of the female community, which may be applied with equal success to the ladies of the present day, I think! And it must be remembered that anyone over thirty in those days was classed as 'old'.

This was a delightful period of children's literature. At last, publishers were producing books for children's pleasure and entertainment, and not just educational and religious reading matter. The limerick verses, like so many others, were designed to give pure enjoyment, and to ignite the spontaneous sense of fun that every child possesses.

Two years later another book of nursery limericks was published, this time by John Marshall and Son entitled *Anecdotes and Adventures of Fifteen Gentlemen*. Again the author is unknown. Again the original copies are scarce, but the Osborne collection houses one.

Here are all *Fifteen Gentleman* —

As a little fat man of Bombay
Was smoking one very hot day,
A bird called a Snipe,
Flew away with his pipe,
Which vex'd the fat man of Bombay.

There was a rich Squire of Southwark,
From morning to night did his mouth work,
So much and so fast,
That he greatly surpass'd,
Westminster, London and Southwark.

There was a poor man of Jamaica,
He'd open'd a shop as a baker;
The nice biscuits he made
Procured him much trade,
With the little black boys of Jamaica.

There was an old captain of Dover,
Whom all the physicians gave over;
  At the sound of the drum
  And "The enemy's come"
Up jump'd the bold captain of Dover.

There was an old merchant at Malta,
Very cross but too stubborn to alter,
  He flew in a rage
  With poor Dr Sage,
Who attended sick people at Malta.

There was a young man at St Kitts,
Who was very much troubled with fits;
  An eclipse of the moon
  Threw him into a swoon;
Alas! poor young man of St Kitts.

A Tailor who sailed from Quebec,
In a storm ventur'd once upon deck,
  But the waves of the sea,
  Were as strong as could be,
And he tumbled in up to his neck.

There was a sick man of Tobago,
Liv'd long on rice-gruel and sago;
  But at last to his bliss,
  The physician said this —
"To a roast leg of mutton you may go."

An old gentleman living at Harwich,
At ninety was thinking of marriage,
  In came his grandson,
  Who was just twenty-one,
And went off with the bride in his carriage.

A butcher there was at Athlone,
Whom a beggar once ask'd for a bone;
  But drove him away
  With a blow of his tray —
O! his heart was as hard as a stone.

There was an Old Miser at Reading,
Had a house, with a yard with a shed in,
'Twas meant for a cow,
But so small that I vow,
The poor creature could scarce gets its head in.

Said a very proud Farmer at Rye-gate,
When the Squire rode up to his high gate,
With your horse and your hound,
You had better go round,
For, I say, you shan't jump over my gate.

There was an old soldier of Bicester,
Was walking one day with his sister,
A bull, with one poke,
Toss'd her into an oak,
Before the old gentleman miss'd her.

A merry old man of Oporto,
Had long had the gout in his fore toe;
And oft when he spoke
To relate a good joke,
A terrible twinge cut it short O!

A lively old man of Madeira,
Thought that wine of the heart was a cheerer,
He often would say,
"Put the bottle this way —
Absent friends! — and I wish they were nearer."

I have arranged the verses presented in this book to show that the last nine have a differing rhyme scheme in the last line. The other six repeat the first line rhyme in the last. I think that the rhyming patterns are quite ingenious even by today's standards. And they certainly showed marked improvements over *The Wonderful Old Women* rhymes.

Many people will be surprised, I am sure, to find some old favourites among this collection. I had never realised, for instance, that 'The Old Soldier from Bicester' originated in this way.

These two humorous little books measuring only 4" x 6" were great favourites with all children and it is not surprising that owing to constant use and wear and tear, not many have survived. But it is thought that a copy of *Anecdotes and Adventures* made its way into the schoolroom at Knowsley Hall, and one verse in particular, 'The Sick Man of Tobago' caught the fancy of a very famous gentleman — as we shall see in the next chapter.

MONUMENT ERECTED OVER THE GRAVE OF ANDREW MCCRATH — 'THE MERRY PEDLAR'
KILMALLOCK, CO. LIMERICK, 1970
Photograph: *Limerick Leader Ltd.*

EDWARD LEAR
1812–1888
Photograph: *National Portrait Gallery*

5

How Pleasant to Know Mr Lear

The life of Edward Lear (1812–1888), the man who promoted and popularised in Britain the nonsense verse now known as the limerick is a fascinating one.

He came from a rather large family which fell on hard times when the father, a naturalised Dane, lost his fortune and was sent to King's Bench prison. The comfortable house at Highgate, with its many servants and carriages, had to be disposed of and Edward went to live in very simple lodgings with his favourite sister, Anne. She was twenty-one years older than he, and spent most of her life looking after her younger brother. The rest of the family were scattered, never to be united again.

Edward was a delicate child, and suffered from bronchitis and asthma. What is worse, he was epileptic, and often had as many as sixteen attacks in a month. He called this the 'terrible demon', as indeed it was, and those dark days were marked by a cross in his diary.

But his infirmities played a large part in shaping his character. He was able to appreciate fully and made the most of periods when he was in good health. He also developed, through his own suffering, a gentleness and understanding for others which remained with him until he died. This probably explains why he had such a fantastic number of friends. Also, of course, he had a marvellous sense of humour that attracted children of all ages.

Lear was a brilliant artist, and when only seventeen he received a commission to paint parrots at the London zoo. Lord Derby, who had a private zoo of his own was very impressed by Lear's work, and invited him to stay at Knowsley Hall, his country estate, near Liverpool, to paint his animals.

He spent four years in all at Lord Derby's residence, and they proved to be some of the happiest years of his life. He met and made friends with many intellectual people, who were impressed by his drawings and other attributes. As well as being an artist, he could compose very entertaining poems and sing songs. It was clear that he had a flair in this direction, too.

A friend, we do not know who, attracted his attention to 'There was a Sick Man of

Tobago', as having an interesting verse form. It was one of the many nursery limericks published in *Anecdotes and Adventures of Fifteen Gentlemen*, as mentioned in the previous chapter, and we do not know for sure whether Lear himself actually saw the first collection in print.

What we do know is that Edward Lear was soon composing and illustrating his own nonsense verses on the same pattern, much to the delight of Lord Derby's grandchildren and their friends and relatives.

Although Lear enjoyed the cultural environment and the companionship of many important people at Knowsley, the conventional way of life and the conversation of the social round sometimes irked him, and he would be glad to escape to the nursery where he was very well received and loved. Here he could relax, and the humorous side of his character could be shown to the full without criticism — he was known to dance a jig and stand on his head when the mood took him. He began to develop his nonsense verses, purely for the amusement of the children. They were not originally intended for publication, and it was not until years later, in 1846, that these verses were collected and published — dedicated to the grandchildren of Lord Derby. Even then, many people did not believe that Lear had written the verses, and thought that in reality they were the work of Lord Derby. This annoyed Lear, for although he never had much to say about his 'nonsense', his close friends believed that it was very dear to his heart.

But Lear's main life's work was landscape painting. He was, indeed one time, drawing master to Queen Victoria. Fairly recently H. I. Brock wrote this verse —

There once was an artist named Lear,
Who wrote verses to make children cheer,
  Though they never made sense,
  Their success was immense,
And the Queen thought Lear was a dear.

Because of ill health he spent most of his life in the Mediterranean area. He had to work very hard for a living, depending entirely on selling his paintings, and the remuneration from his books for finances. He had many influential good friends who at one time or another came to his aid when money was scarce.

Lear always considered himself a very plain man, and would write derogatory verses about his appearance. I have a feeling that being such a lover of beauty, his own face and general appearance constantly irritated him, and the nonsense verses helped to relieve the tension.

This is the way he described himself 'By Way of Preface' —

How pleasant to know Mr Lear!
Who has written such volumes of stuff,
Some think him ill-tempered and queer,
But few think him pleasant enough.

His mind is concrete and fastidious,
His nose is remarkably big;
His visage is more or less hideous,
His beard it resembles a wig.

He has ears, and two eyes, and ten fingers,
Leastways if you reckon two thumbs;
Long ago he was one of the singers,
But now he is one of the dumbs.

He sits in a beautiful parlour,
With hundreds of books on the wall,
He drinks a great deal of Marsala,
And never gets tipsy at all.

He has many friends, laymen and clerical,
Old Foss is the name of his cat;
His body is perfectly spherical,
He weareth a runcible hat.

When he walks in a waterproof white,
The children run after him so!
Calling out, "He's come in his night-
Gown, that crazy old Englishman, oh!"

He weeps by the side of the ocean,
He weeps on the top of the hill;
He purchases pancakes and lotion,
And chocolate shrimps from the mill.

He reads but he cannot speak Spanish,
He cannot abide ginger-beer;
Ere the days of his pilgrimage vanish,
How pleasant to know Mr Lear!

When the first *Book of Nonsense* was published in 1846 it was an immediate success. Ten years later another edition was printed, and this time Lear did not put his name to it. Instead, inside the front cover was the verse —

There was an old Derry down Derry,
Who loved to see little folks merry,
So he made them a Book,
And with laughter they shook,
At the fun of that Derry down Derry.

In 1861 it was decided to bring out another edition with new verses, limerick style, and drawings under the author's name. The edition sold two thousand copies, and Lear wanted to sell the copyright.

He received £125 for it, and that is all the money he ever earned out of his *Book of Nonsense*, apart from the first two editions which were not large. He thought he had made a bargain and put the money into the bank with great gusto. The book went to nearly thirty editions in his lifetime, and has sold countless thousands of copies since.

The last few years of his life were spent at the Villa Emily in San Remo, Italy. Lear had never married and his only companions were his two native manservants and his cat, Foss, who lived to the great age of seventeen, and died only a few months before his own death, in February 1888. The graves of both Edward Lear and his cat can be seen at San Remo.

Lear was still endeavouring to illustrate Tennyson's poems, when he suffered his last illness. Tennyson and his family had been close friends of his, and the task to which he had set himself had followed him for much of his life.

But it is not for his paintings that Lear is remembered today. It is his nonsense verses, and others such as 'The Owl and the Pussycat' and 'The Jumblies', that have found their niche in classical literature.

This is how Langford Reed, of whom we shall hear more later, summed up Lear's work —

A goddess, capricious in Fame,
You may strive to make noted your name,
But she either neglects you
Or coolly selects you
For laurels distinct from your aim.

There was a part of Lear that never grew up, and he remembered his own feelings of childhood, which is so important when dealing with children.

All young people felt drawn to this fun-loving man the twinkling eyes, who always had such comical things to relate. I think it was Lear's love of children that promoted the growth of this nonsense verse in his own mind. 'The Sick Man of Tobago' snowballed into many, many verses about all sorts of queer people. This was Lear's luxury. The precious leisure time spent composing nonsense, acted as a soothing balm easing out tensions of the everyday fight for survival, and put all things into proportion.

Lear was a clever man. In his kindly way his nonsense ridiculed the Victorian way of life with its class distinctions and petty conventions. But none of his rhymes contained malice or were in any way satirical, and the only derogatory ones were against himself. Here lies the secret of their success. For it was easy to appreciate. It offended no one, and pleased many. Lear was one of the few writers who introduced laughter into the rather sombre homes of the nineteenth century, and his clever illustrations which accompanied the verses helped to establish the images of fun.

It must in fact, have been very pleasant to know Mr Lear, and I for one, would have liked to have had that honour.

Although Lear's verses have never been classified, as such, it seems to me that they did reflect his own personality and way of life, to a certain extent. Working on this, rightly or wrongly, I now present some of his 'learics' to illustrate this point

As I have mentioned, Edward Lear was a lover of beauty and was often distressed by his own appearance. This is the way he saw himself—

There was an old man in a tree,
Whose whiskers were lovely to see;
But the birds of the air, pluck'd them perfectly bare,
To make themselves nests in that tree.

There was an Old Man on whose nose,
Most birds of the air could repose,
But they all flew away, at the closing of day,
Which relieved that Old Man and his nose.

There was an Old Man in a barge,
Whose nose was exceedingly large;
But in fishing by night,
It supported a light,
Which helped that Old Man in a barge.

There was an Old Man of West Dumpet,
Who possessed a large nose like a trumpet;
When he blew it aloud,
It astonished the crowd,
And was heard through the whole of West Dumpet.

There was an old person of Cassel,
Whose nose finished off in a tassel;
But they called out "Oh well,
Don't it look like a bell,"
Which perplexed that old person of Cassel.

There was an Old Man with a nose,
Who said "If you choose to suppose,
That my nose is too long
You are certainly wrong!"
That remarkable Man with a nose.

There was an Old Man with a beard,
Who said "It is just as I feared! —
Two Owls and a Hen, four Larks and a Wren,
Have all built their nests in my beard!"

Lear's infirmities often plunged him into despair —

There was an Old Person of Buda,
Whose conduct grew ruder and ruder,
Till at last with a hammer,
They silenced his clamour,
By smashing that Person of Buda.

There was an Old Man of Cape Horn,
Who wished he had never been born;
So he sat on a chair, till he died of despair,
That dolorous Man of Cape Horn.

There was an Old Person of Rheims,
Who was troubled with horrible dreams;
So to keep him awake
They fed him on cake,
Which amused that Old Person of Rheims.

Other times he felt very fit and happy —

There was an Old Man of the Isles,
Whose face was pervaded with smiles;
He sung high dum diddle,
And played on the fiddle,
That amiable man of the Isles.

There was an Old Person of Skye,
Who waltzed with a bluebottle fly;
They buzzed a sweet tune,
To the light of the moon,
And entranced all the people of Skye.

Although Lear travelled a great deal, he was not a good sailor, and sea crossings were always a great trial to him. I think these verses bear this out —

The was an Old Man in a boat
Who said "I'm afloat, I'm afloat,"
When they said "No you ain't,"
He was ready to faint,
That unhappy Old Man in a boat.

There was an old person of Grange,
Whose manners were scroobious and strange;
He sailed to St Blubb, in a waterproof tub,
That aquatic old person of Grange.

When preparing to go on one of his expeditions, 'The Old Man of Coblenz' may have been wishful thinking!

There was an Old Man of Coblenz,
The length of whose legs was immense;
He went with one prance, from Turkey to France,
That surprising Old Man of Coblenz.

One of Lear's favourite pastimes was painting birds, and so it is not surprising that this interest is shown in his 'nonsense'.

There was an Old Man of Dumblane,
Who greatly resembled a crane;
But they said — "It is wrong
Since your legs are so long,
To request you won't stay in Dumblane?"

There was an old person of Nice,
Whose associates were usually Geese,
They walked out together, in all sorts of weather,
That affable person of Nice!

There was an old man of El Hums;
Who lived upon nothing but crumbs;
Which he picked off the ground,
With other birds round,
In the roads and the lanes of El Hums.

At various villas in the Mediterranean area, Lear craved to be left alone, and not be troubled by sightseers who often invaded his privacy. When not working he loved to potter in his garden, and was often very annoyed to find strangers there, curious to catch a glimpse of him. This verse almost certainly refers to these instances.

There was an Old Man in a garden,
Who always begged everyone's pardon;
When they asked him "What for?"
He replied "You're a bore,
And trust you'll go out of my garden."

There was only one verse that Edward Lear wrote that was generally accepted to be directly concerned with someone. This 'someone' was Gladstone, whom Lear did not like, and who had the reputation of delivering speeches at railway stations.

There was an Old Man at a Station,
Who made a promiscuous oration;
But they said "Take some snuff,
You've talked quite enough,
You afflicting Old Man of the Station."

The frustration that Lear felt about the Victorian way of life, and its rigid behaviour pattern is illustrated in the following, I feel —

There was an Old Man of Whitehaven,
Who danced a quadrille with a Raven;
But they said "It's absurd,
To encourage this bird,"
So they smashed that Old Man of Whitehaven.

There was an old man of Thermopylæ,
Who never did anything properly;
But they said, "If you choose, To boil eggs in your shoes,
You shall never remain in Thermopylæ."

There was an Old Man of Hong Kong
Who never did anything wrong;
He lay on his back,
With his head in a sack,
That innocuous Man of Hong Kong.

There was a young person in green,
Who seldom was fit to be seen;
She wore a long shawl,
Over bonnet and all,
Which enveloped that person in green.

There was an old person of Chili,
Whose conduct was painfully silly;
He sat on the stairs,
Eating apples and pears,
That imprudent Old Person of Chili.

This verse is reminiscent of 'The Old Woman of France' featured in the very first English limerick book, and makes me wonder whether in fact, Lear saw this collection as well as 'The Sick Man of Tobago'.

There was an old lady of France,
Who taught little ducklings to dance;
When she said, "Tick-a-tack",
They only said "Quack",
Which grieved that Old Lady of France.

This is the original 'Old Man of Calcutta' —

There was an Old Man of Calcutta,
Who perpetually ate bread and butter;
Till a great bit of muffin, on which he was stuffing,
Choked that horrid old man of Calcutta.

This was quickly taken up by Sir W. S. Gilbert, as we shall see later on —

There was an Old Man in a tree,
Who was horribly bored by a bee;
When they said "Does it buzz?"
He replied "Yes it does!
It's a regular brute of a Bee!"

I have found four of Lear's verses that have a differing last line, but there may be more —

There was an Old Lady whose folly,
Induced her to sit in a holly;
Whereon by a thorn, her dress being torn,
She quickly became melancholy.

There was an Old Man of the coast,
Who placidly sat on a post;
But when it was cold,
He relinquished his hold,
And called for some hot buttered toast.

There was an Old Man who supposed,
That the street door was partially closed;
But some very large rats,
Ate his coats and his hats,
While that futile old gentleman dozed.

There was a Young Lady whose eyes,
Were unique as to colour and size,
When she opened them wide,
People turned aside,
And started away in surprise.

The rest of Lear's limericks as presented here, just illustrate his marvellous sense of fun.

There was an Old Man of Kilkenny,
Who never had more than a penny;
He spent all that money,
In onions and honey,
That wayward old man of Kilkenny.

There was a Young Lady whose chin,
Resembled the point of a pin;
So she had it made sharp,
And purchased a harp,
And played several tunes with her chin.

There was an Old Man of Vesuvious,
Who studied the works of Vitruvius;
When the flames burnt his book, to drinking he took,
That morbid Old Man of Vesuvius.

There was an Old Man of Wrekin,
Whose shoes made a horrible creaking,
But they said "Tell us whether
Your shoes are of leather,
Or of what, you Old Man of Wrekin?"

There was an old Lady of Chertsey,
Who made a remarkable curtsey;
She twirled round and round,
Till she sunk to the ground,
Which distressed all the people of Chertsey.

There was an Old Man who when little,
Fell casually into a kettle,
But growing too stout,
He could never get out,
So he passed all his life in that kettle.

There was a Young Girl of Majorca,
Whose aunt was a very fast walker;
She walked seventy miles,
And leaped fifteen stiles,
Which astonished that Girl of Majorca.

There was an Old Person of Tring,
Who embellished his nose with a ring;
He gazed at the moon, every evening in June.
That ecstatic Old Person of Tring.

There was an Old Man on some rocks,
Who shut his wife up in a box,
When she said "Let me out", he exclaimed, "Without doubt,
You will pass all your life in that box."

There was an Old Man of Berlin,
Whose form was uncommonly thin;
Till he once by mistake,
Was mixed up in a cake,
So they baked that Old Man of Berlin.

There was a young lady of Firle,
Whose hair was addicted to curl;
It curled up a tree, and all over the sea,
That expansive young lady of Firle.

There was an old person of Putney,
Whose food was roast spiders and chutney.
Which he took with his tea,
Within sight of the sea,
That romantic old person of Putney.

There was an old person of Deal
Who in walking, used only his heel;
When they said, "Tell us why?" — He made no reply;
That mysterious old person of Deal.

6
The Others

I AM well satisfied that Lear did not know of the word 'limerick' as a description of the nonsense verse that he had made so famous. In Ireland it had been known as such since the era of the Maigue Poets, but in Britain it was not labelled the same until 1898. I can well remember asking at school why the limerick was so called. The reply, "no one knows," has been echoed in all text books dealing with this subject before and since. It is reasonable to suppose, therefore, that the word 'limerick' crept into the English language through Irish connections, as mentioned in a former chapter.

After the success of Lear's nonsense verses, everyone from Tennyson downwards began to compose limericks. The poet and the layman alike, had at last found common ground. Here was a verse form that was universally understood and appreciated. Used as an entertainment, it blossomed out, and some clever and comical verses were composed.

Charles Lutwidge Dodgson, better known as Lewis Carroll, was a contemporary of Lear's and his humour and style were similar. In his works *Alice in Wonderland, Alice Through the Looking-Glass*, and many more, Lewis Carroll showed the world his sense of fun and deep understanding of children. He also wrote limericks.

This one was composed for the amusement of a child called Miss Vera Bellinger, a great friend of his —

There was a young lady of station,
"I love man" was her sole Exclamation;
But when men cried "You flatter"
She replied "Oh no matter,
Isle of Man is the true explanation."

These are entitled 'Melodies' —

There was an old farmer of Reedall,
Who made holes in his face with a needle;
Then went far deeper in,
Than to pierce through the skin,
And strange to say, he was made a beadle.

There was an eccentric old draper,
Who wore a hat made of paper;
It went to a point
Yet it looked out of joint,
The cause of which he said was "vapour."

There was once a man of Oporta,
Who daily got shorter and shorter.
The reason he said,
Was the hod on his head,
Which was filled with the heaviest mortar.

His sister named Lucy O'Finner,
Grew constantly thinner and thinner;
The reason was plain
She slept in the rain,
And never was allowed any dinner.

This world famous limerick is also attributed to Lewis Carroll, who composed it to entertain a dinner party that he was attending —

There was a young lady of Niger,
Who smiled as she rode on a tiger;
They came back from the ride,
With the lady inside,
And the smile on the face of the tiger.

Andrew Lang, that much loved Scottish poet and classical scholar, is remembered today, primarily for his children's collections of fairy stories — *The Green Fairy Book, The Blue Fairy Book*, etc. He also wrote limericks —

There was a young lady of Limerick,
Who stole from a farmer named Tim a rick,

When the priest at the alter,
Suggested a halter,
She fled from the county of Limerick.

There was an auld birkie ca'ed Milton,
Who lo'ed na the lads wi' a kilt on;
Gie'd Gillespie a rasp,
Ca'd Gillespie "Galasp"
Sae slicht was the Gaelic he built on.

Sir William S. Gilbert was also very fond of the limerick form, and many are published in his book *Bab Ballads*. Here is an early one, but the last line does not scan properly.

Of Agib, who amid Tartaric scenes,
Wrote a lot of ballet music in his teens.
His gentle spirit rolls
In a melody of souls,
Which is pretty, but I don't know what it means.

Here is a double stanza as set to music by Sir Arthur Sullivan and sung at a tongue twisting pace in *The Yeoman of the Guard* —

A man who would woo a fair maid,
Should prentice himself to a trade,
And study all day,
In a methodical way,
How to flatter, cajole and persuade.

He should prentice himself at fourteen,
And practise from morning to e'en,
And when he's of age,
If he will, I'll engage,
He may capture the heart of a queen.

It is purely a matter of skill,
Which all may attain if they will
  But every Jack
  Must study the knack
If he wants to make sure of his Jill!

The best known limerick song of Gilbert's must be the one from *The Sorcerer*, first performed in 1877.

Oh, my name is John Wellington Wells,
I'm a dealer in magic and spells,
  In blessings and curses,
  And ever-filled purses,
In prophecies, witches and knells.

If you want a proud foe to 'make tracks' —
If you'd melt a rich uncle in wax —
  You've but to look in
  On our resident Djinn,
Number seventy, Simmery Axe.

Gilbert could not resist having a stab at the offbeat —

There was an old man of St Bees,
Who was stung in the arm by a wasp,
When asked "Does it hurt?"
He replied "No it doesn't,
I'm so glad it wasn't a hornet."

One of the earliest men to name this form of verse, a limerick, was Rudyard Kipling, who mentioned it in his work *Stalky*, in the early 1880s.
He also wrote a limerick which goes —

There was a young boy of Quebec,
Who fell in the ice to his neck'
  When asked "Are you friz?"
  He replied "Yes, I is,
But we don't call this cold in Quebec."

Robert Louis Stevenson wrote this one —

There was an old man of the Cape,
Who made himself garments of crepe,
When asked "Do they tear?"
He replied "Here and there,
But they're perfectly splendid for shape."

Mark Twain, author of *Huckleberry Finn*, produced this one —

A man hired by John Smith and Co.
Loudly declared he would tho.
  Man that he saw
  Dumping dirt near his store
The drivers, therefore, didn't do.

Once President of the USA, Mr Woodrow Wilson, was fond of limericks. He wrote these two, and they must be regarded as classics —

As a beauty, I'm not a great star,
There are others more handsome by far,
  But my face, I don't mind it,
  Because I'm behind it,
'Tis the folks in the front, that I jar.

I sat next to the Duchess at tea;
It was just as I feared it would be;
  Her rumblings abdominal
  Were truly phenominal,
And everyone thought it was me!

Another American, Joseph Kennedy, father of the famous Kennedy brothers wrote this one after The Great War —

Says the Frenchman, "You'll pay us for sure."
Says the German, "We can't, for we're poor."
  So Fritz with a whine
  Sings his 'Watch on the Rhine',
But Poilu sings, 'Watch on the Ruhr'.

Nobel prize winner, Betrand Russell gave us this —

There was a young girl of Shanghai,
Who was so exceedingly shy,
  That undressing at night
  She turned out the light
For fear of the All-Seeing Eye.

Another Nobel prize winner for literature, was John Galsworthy of *Forsyte Saga* fame. He contributed this stanza —

To an artist a husband named Bicket
Said "Turn your backside and I'll kick it,
  You have painted my wife
  In the nude to the life,
Do you think for a moment, that's cricket?"

Oliver Wendell Holmes, 1809-1894, a doctor of medicine and a well known wit, wrote a limerick which has come to be regarded as a classic —

The Reverend Henry Ward Beecher,
Called a hen a most elegant creature,
  The hen pleased with that,
  Laid an egg in his hat —
And thus did the hen reward Beecher.

Edward Bradley (Cuthbert Bede) wrote this gem in 1972 —

There was a queer fellow called Woodin
Who always ate pepper with puddin',
  Till one day, 'tis said,
  He sneezed off his head!
That imprudent old fellow named Woodin.

Arthur Clement Hilton was a student at Cambridge, and published limericks in a rare magazine called *The Light Green*, of which only two issues materialised in 1872. As Mr Hilton was only twenty-six when he died, it is not surprising that most of his verses are about university life. He has been described as a young genius, by people who knew him. Here are some of his limericks —

There was a young genius of Queen's,
Who was fond of explosive machines.
  He once blew up a door,
  But he'll do it no more,
For it chanced that the door was the Dean's.

There was a young gourmand of John's,
Who'd a notion of dining on swans,
  To The Backs he took nets
  To capture the cygnets,
But was told they were kept for the Dean.

There was an old fellow of Trinity,
A Doctor well versed in Divinity,
  But he took to free thinking
  And then to deep drinking,
And so had to leave the vicinity.

Thomas Anstey Guthrie wrote this in 1907 —

There was an old man of Bengal,
Who purchased a bat and a ball,
  Some gloves and some pads;
  It was one of his fads,
For he never played cricket at all.

Gelett Burgess, the American writer composed this piece of nonsense in 1914 —

I wish that my room had a floor!
I don't care so much for a door,
  But this crawling around
  Without touching the ground,
Is getting to be quite a bore!

Dixon Lanier Merritt, a Florida newspaper man, was responsible for this classic —

A wonderful bird is the pelican ;
His bill can hold more than his belican.
  He can take in his beak
  Food enough for a week,
But I'm damned if I see how the helican!

Edward Valpy Knox, once editor of *Punch* contributed this —

There was a young curate of Hants,
Who suddenly took off his pants;
  When asked why he did,
  He replied "To get rid,
Of this regular army of ants."

Eugene Field who died in 1895 was a journalist and theatre critic for many years. He also wrote memorable limericks —

'Tis strange how the newspapers honor
A creature that's called prima donna,
They say not a thing
Of how she can sing.
But write of the clothes she has on her.

Now what in the world shall we dioux
With the bloody and murderous Sioux.
Who some time ago
Took an arrow and bow,
And raised such a hellabelioux?'

This started off a flair for using spelling rhymes — included in Carolyn Wells' *A Whimsey Anthology.*

A wandering tribe called the Siouxs
Wear moccasins, having no shiouxs.
They are made of buckskin,
With the fleshy side in,
Embroidered with beads of bright hyiouxs.

The principal food of the Siouxs
Is Indian maize, which they briouxs.
And hominy make,
Or mix in a cake,
And eat it with forks, as they chïouxs.

Dante Gabriel Rossetti was a much revered poet, and he also turned his hand to limericks, which probably are not quite so successful as his poetry.

There was a combative artist named Whistler
Who is, like his own hog hairs, a bristler;
A tube of white lead
And a punch on the head
Offer varied attractions to Whistler.

There's a Portugese person named Howell
Who lays on his lies with a trowell;
Should he give over lying,
Twill be when he's dying,
For living is dying with Howell.

There was an old he-wolf named Gamart,
Beware of him if thou as lamb art;
  Else thy tail and thy toes
  And thine innocent nose
Will be ground by the grinders of Gamart.

There was a poor chap called Rossetti;
As a painter with many kicks met he —
  With more as a man —
  But sometimes he ran,
And that saved the rear of Rossetti.

Here is a popular limerick written by Archibald Marshall in 1904 —

There was a young man of Devizes,
Whose ears were of different sizes;
  The one that was small
  Was no good at all,
But the other won several prizes.

George du Maurier, the celebrated writer wrote limericks in a kind of pigeon French with rather quaint results —

A Potsdam, les totaux absteneurs,
Comme tant d'autres titotalleurs,
  Sont gloutons, omnivores,
  Nasorubicolores,
Grand manchons, et terrible duffeurs.

Chaque epoque a ses grands noms sonores;
Or, de tous les defunts cockolores,
  Le moral Fenelon,
  Michel Ange et Johnson
(Le Docteur), sont les plus awful bores!

Entertainers, too, often wrote limericks. Here is one engendered by George Robey — that famous music hall comedian. He had many on his list —

An eccentric old person of Slough,
Who took all his meals with a cow,
  Always said "It's uncanny,
  She's so like Aunt Fanny"
But he never would indicate how.

Eille Norwood was an actress of renown and lived from 1861 to 1948. Here is one of her efforts —

A pretty young actress, a stammerer,
Knew acting in theatres would damn her. A
  Producer (film genius)
  Engaged her as 'Venus' —
The rest of the story's 'in camera'.

Charles Coburn, the veteran singer of 'The Man who Broke the Bank of Monte Carlo' and 'Two lovely Black Eyes' wrote this —

A charming young lady called Nelly
  Once danced herself almost to a jelly;
  The doctors declared
  That her life might be spared
If she stayed for a week at Pwllheli.

Here is a verse attributed to the pen of H. G. Wells —

Mr Wells of the big Cerebellum,
Uses mountains of paper or vellum;
  When his temper gets bad,
  And we ask "Why go mad?"
He replies, "They don't do as I tell 'em."

And another —

Our novels get longa and longa;
Their language gets stronga and stronga.
There is much to be said
For life that is led,
In illiterate places like Bonga.

Arnold Bennett, that celebrated writer who lived from 1867-1931 contributed this verse —

There was a young man of Montrose,
Who had pockets in none of his clothes,
  And when asked by his lass
  Where he carried his brass,
He said "Darling, I pay through the nose!"

William Dean Inge, the Dean of St Paul's Cathedral from 1911 to 1934, was by all accounts a gloomy and pessimistic man. His hobby of composing limericks brought a little light relief to his life! Here is one that has been quoted as the perfect limerick —

There was an old man of Khartoum,
Who kept two tame sheep in his room.
  "To remind him," he said
  "Of two friends who were dead!"
But he could not remember of whom.

In Britain and America limericks were very soon sung as were the first Irish stanzas. In Britain the tune used was 'The Spanish Nobilio', and in America they used 'The Gay Caballero'.

Limerick songs were popular at Scout and Guide Camps, Youth Clubs and in fact in all gatherings where the 'sing-song' was used as a form of entertainment.

The pattern is still used today, but not to such a great extent. Each participant sings his limerick solo, and in between each verse everyone joins in the chorus which goes —

That was a beautiful rhyme,
Sing us another one
Just like the other one —
Sing us another one do.

Here are some old favourites, too good to leave out, which have stood the test of time.

There was a young workman whose creed,
Was wholly untainted by greed.
  More work for more pay
  He considered fair play,
But nobody followed his lead.

There was a young lady of Ryde,
Who ate a green apple and died;
  The apple fermented
  Inside the lamented
And made cider, inside her inside.

There was a young lady of Kent,
Who said that she knew what it meant
  When men asked her to dine,
  Gave cocktails and wine,
She knew what it meant — and she went.

There was a young lady of Lynn,
Who was so uncommonly thin,
  That when she essayed
  To drink lemonade,
She slipped through the straw and fell in.

An epicure dining at Crewe,
Found quite a large mouse in his stew,
  Said the waiter "Don't shout
  And wave it about!
Or the rest will be wanting one too!"

There was once a man of Bengal,
Who was asked to a fancy dress ball;
  He murmured "I'll risk it,
  And go as a biscuit";
But the dog ate him up in the hall.

There was an old man of Blackheath,
Who sat on his set of false teeth.
  Said he with a start
  "Oh Lord bless my heart,
I've bitten myself underneath."

There was an old man of Peru,
Who dreamt he was eating his shoe.
  He woke in the night,
  In a terrible fright,
And found it was perfectly true!

There was a young lady of Flint,
Who had the most horrible squint.
  She could scan the whole sky
  With her uppermost eye,
While the other was reading small print.

There once were two cats of Kilkenny,
Each thought there was one cat too many.
  So they fought and they fit,
  And they scratched and they bit,
Till instead of two cats there weren't any.

There was a young lady called Starky,
Who had an affair with a darky;
  The result of her sins
  Was quadruplets — not twins,
One black, one white, and two khaki.

They say I was in my youth,
Uncouth and ungainly, forsooth!
  I can only reply,
  "'Tis a lie, 'tis a lie!
I was couth — I was perfectly couth."

There was a young fellow called Green
Whose musical sense was not keen,
  He said "It's most odd
  But I cannot tell God
Save the Weasel from Pop goes the Queen!"

There was an old person of Lyme
Who married three wives at a time,
  When asked "Why a third?"
  He replied "One's absurd,
And bigamy, sir, is a crime."

There was a faith healer of Deal,
Who said "Although pain isn't real,
  If I sit on a pin
  And it punctures my skin,
I dislike what I fancy I feel."

At the turn of the century, and in the years that followed, the limerick enjoyed its heyday. The Edwardian Era may well be described as The Limerick Era. They were quoted everywhere especially on the Stock Exchange where they became unprintable and traditionally 'blue'. Magazines and journals ran competitions, and the public racked their brains to think of originals.

After The Great War, the limerick seemed to lose all respectability, and the very word became taboo with ordinary folk — until one man rescued it from the mire into which it had sunk, and restored it, to a great extent, to its original level in literature.

The progress and development of the limerick through the years owes much to Mr Herbert Langford Reed, as we shall see in the next chapter.

7

THERE WAS A YOUNG FELLOW NAMED REED

A YEAR after the death of Edward Lear, another man destined to shape the future of the limerick verse, was born. He was, as mentioned earlier, Herbert Langford Reed, who came from a middle-class Victorian family, and although not rich, never lacked for the material things of life.

He was educated privately, at Clapham Collegiate and Hove College. His childhood was essentially a happy one, and this fact together with his marked sense of humour must explain his happy-go-lucky attitude to life.

Reed quickly realised that his interests lay in journalism and at the age of twenty-one he joined the editorial staff of the *Daily Mail*. He saw active service, in the First World War, in France in 1917, and was official editor of Government propaganda films sent abroad in 1918. His first book *The Chronicles of Charlie* was published in 1916, and from then onwards he never looked back.

After the war he again threw himself into writing, and among his many works were scripts for some of the first Charlie Chaplin films.

He married Hetty Spiers, and they had one daughter, Joan. Both his wife and his daughter dabbled in painting and sketching, and the latter spent some time on the stage. All three were lovers of the arts, and lived in a pleasant but impractical world of their own making.

Mr Trevor Bailey, the cricketer, was a nephew of Langford Reed, as his mother was Reed's sister. In a letter to me, Mr Bailey described his uncle as a man of medium height, with a remarkable sense of fun. He well remembered the Reeds' house in St John's Wood, as one littered with books, and generally gloriously untidy — but with a carefree, happy atmosphere that could not be surpassed.

In the early 1920s Reed saw the great need for a revival and general cleansing of the limerick form. He realised that its original potential was in danger of being annihilated by the recent reputation thrust upon it.

He decided to collect authored limericks, and those from the oral collection, and present them, together with his own compositions in *The Complete Limerick Book*.

This work was published in Britain in 1924, and in America the following year. It was an instant success, and went to five editions.

Here is the preamble to the book —

> There was a young fellow named Reed,
> Who said "There's a need, a great need,
> For a limerick book."
> So he made one — and look,
> Here's the book that he made, now proceed.

George Bernard Shaw, himself a great lover of the form remarked that Reed was the only man to write clean limericks at that time, and so saved the verse from extinction. In fact his work may be described this way —

> Langford Reed saved the limerick verse,
> From being taken away in a hearse.
> He made it so clean
> Now it's fit for a queen,
> Re-established for better or worse.

Reed dedicated his first limerick book to '...the ancient city of Limerick' because, naturally, he had a hunch that the verse must have originated there. He thought that the old Irish song 'Will you come up to Limerick' may have sparked off the new metre. But this theory has since been disproved as the song has no bearing whatsoever on the limerick form.

He also stated that whoever it was who invented the limerick ought to have a statue erected in his memory, as he had provided the world with an inexhaustible source of amusement. Now we have a monument erected in memory of Andrew McCrath, one of the Croom bards who developed the metrical form and gave humour to this type of verse over two hundred years ago. It was unveiled in 1970 at the Maigue festival.

It is obvious that Langford Reed knew nothing of the Maigue Poets, or of the first English nursery limericks. However he does give a clear picture in his book of the Great Boom of 1907–8 and of the many competitions that followed. He relates that the country went crazy on limericks at that time. Nearly every newspaper and magazine ran competitions with large prizes. There was a boom in rhyming dictionaries. The Post Office reported a fantastic number of 6*d* postal orders sold, being the entrance fee for most contests — at one time as many as fourteen times the normal quantity!

London Opinion magazine fielded the forerunner of the nationwide contests, and set a standard for other papers.

Here is an example of one competition in which the paper gave the first four lines —

There was a young lady of Ryde
Whose locks were considerably dyed,
  The hue of her hair
  Made everyone stare —

And the two winning lines were —

"She's piebald, she'll die bald!" they cried.
And "My locks seem magnetic," she cried.

The prizes offered were substantial even by today's standards. Some offered £3 a week for life, a new house, large money prizes — and all for clean limericks!

Some allegations of unfair selections were fought in the courts. And the Anti-Gambling League took umbrage at the limerick competitions saying that they did not do the morals of the country any good! This was nonsense of course, as anything won on merit could not be considered gambling.

The limerick contest king in the commercial world was in those days Mr Samuda, the well-known tobacco merchant. There was no entrance fee — only a cigarette coupon.

This was the first incomplete limerick to be staged —

That the Traylee's the best cigarette,
Is a "tip" that we cannot forget,
  And in buying I'll mention
  There's a three pound a week pension,

This was the winning line sent in by a resident of Cardiff —

"Two good 'lines' — one you give, one you get."

He was awarded £3 a week for life.

After this very successful attempt, the tobacco king staged many more limerick contests with large prizes. Here is another first prize offered —

> *A pretty well-kept country villa standing in its own grounds and decorated and furnished throughout by Waring and Gillow, and containing kitchen, drawing room, dining room, and bedrooms, with everything in it conducive to home comfort. Table linen, crockery, household utensils, bed linen, draperies, are all included. Every modern improvement including bathroom (H&C) and electric light...*

Also, a horse and trap and £2 a week for life went with this prize.

No wonder everyone from the poet laureate downwards was tempted to have a go.

A Scotsman this time submitted the winning line.

Mr Beynon was a champion limerick prize winner over this period, and he wrote the last line to this —

A motorist out on the spree
Said "Speed limits don't bother me."
  So during a trip
  He let the car rip,
And a "full stop" made R.I.P.

This is how Langford Reed defined the essentials of a good limerick:

a. A good last line
b. Ingenuity of rhyme
c. A good plot, creating a ludicrous instance right from the start.
And also the verse must have a strong cause as well as a strong effect.

Langford Reed had a flair for composing comic verse, and wrote hundreds of limericks during his lifetime, and also many more limerick books after the success of his first work.

This is a selection of his own verses from *The Complete Limerick Book* —

There was an old lady of Leith
Who had most remarkable teeth;
  They were not very strong
  But so spiky and long,
That she had to keep each in a sheath.

There was an old man of Bombay,
Who stood on his head all the day;
  In the main thoroughfare
  With his legs in the air,
Soliciting alms by the way.

An indolent vicar of Bray,
His roses allowed to decay;
  His wife more alert,
  Bought a powerful squirt,
And said to her spouse, "Let us spray."

Reed often was tempted to write verses which ridiculed the English way of spelling —

There was a young lady of Slough
Who went for a ride on a cough,
  The brute pitched her off,
  When she started to coff,
She ne'er rides on such animals nough.

This is what he said of Lear's work —

Although at the limericks of Lear,
We may feel tempted to sneer,
  We should never forget
  That we owe him a debt,
For his work as the first pioneer.

This verse refers to the incident after the First World War, when our government entertained the German delegation at the Ritz.

Has our government quite lost its wits
In allotting such quarters to Fritz?
  Would it not have looked better
  While housing a debtor,
To alter its name to "The Writs"?

When asked at a dinner party to make up an impromptu rhyme using Florida, Mr Reed produced this — with apologies!

There was an old person of Florida,
Whose conduct could not have been horrider,
  At his hotel, the waiters,
  He pelted with taters,
And the chambermaids kissed in the corrider!

And here is his suggested epitaph for the tomb of a glutton —

Her lies a poor gluttonous sinner,
Than in life considerably thinner,
  He's gone so they tell
  Without doubt to — well —
To the place where they cook the best dinner!

Here is an unusual piece of frivolity described as a limerick in ten spasms, and entitled 'The Irony of Fate' or 'Why She was Jilted'.

Oh, list to the delorous tale,
Of unfortunate fair Abigail,
  A centipede sweet
  Engaged to discreet
Young Horace, a prosperous snail.

And everyone said re the news,
"What a sensible girl to choose,
  "He's a house of his own
  Freehold, and is known
To be steady and never to booze."

The morn of the marriage arrived
By an effort the bridegroom contrived
  At the church to be there
  With ten minutes to spare
In his laudable haste to be wived.

His "best man" was Sidney the spider
An excellent fellow as guider
  In four pairs of new pants
  With a bunch of choice plants,
For the bride, a bouquet to provide her.

But alack and alas — Where's the bride?
Is she ill? Is she shy? Does she hide?
  Thus queried the guests
  When in spite of all quests
No sign of Miss C. could be spied.

Till, at length, Mr Spider departed,
By the request of the groom, broken hearted,
  To at once take a fly
  And find out just why
She tarried, and if she had started.

When Sidney drove up to her dwelling
He heard a lugubrious yelling,
  And this was the reason
  For such seeming treason
And the tears Abigail was expelling.

OLD WOMAN OF LYNN.

There liv'd an Old Woman at Lynn,
Whose Nose very near touch'd her chin,
You may easy suppose,
She had plenty of Beaux;
This charming Old Woman of Lynn.

OLD WOMAN OF EXETER.

There dwelt an Old Woman at Exeter,
When visitors came it sore vexed her,
So for fear they should eat,
She lock'd up all the meat;
This stingy Old Woman of Exeter.

OLD WOMAN OF HARROW.

There was an Old Woman of Harrow,
Who visited in a Wheel barrow,
And her servant before,
Knock'd loud at each door;
To announce the Old Woman of Harrow.

OLD WOMAN OF GOSPORT.

There was an Old Woman of Gosport,
And she was one of the cross sort,
When she dress'd for the Ball;
Her wig was too small;
Which enrag'd this Old Lady of Gosport.

FROM 'THE HISTORY OF SIXTEEN WONDERFUL OLD WOMEN'
Featured in *Flowers of Delight*
Edited by Leonard de Vries, and published by Dennis Dobson

MISTRESS TOWL.

There was an Old Woman named Towl,
Who went out to Sea with her Owl,
But the Owl was Sea-sick,
And scream'd for Physic;
Which sadly annoy'd Mistress Towl.

OLD WOMAN OF CROYDON.

There was an Old Woman of Croydon,
To look young she affected the Hoyden,
And would jump and would skip,
Till she put out her hip;
Alas poor Old Woman of Croydon.

OLD WOMAN OF BATH.

There was an Old Woman of Bath,
And She was as thin as a Lath,
She was brown as a berry,
With a Nose like a Cherry;
This skinny Old Woman of Bath.

OLD WOMAN OF EALING.

There was an Old Woman of Ealing,
She jump'd till her head touch'd the Ceiling
When 2 1 6 4,
Was announc'd at her Door;
As a prize to th 'Old Woman of Ealing.

FROM 'THE HISTORY OF SIXTEEN WONDERFUL OLD WOMEN'
Featured in *Flowers of Delight*
Edited by Leonard de Vries, and published by Dennis Dobson

The delay in fulfilling her bond
Was because up till now she had donned
  But forty-four shoes
  Of her hundred small "twos"
No wonder her heart did despond.

When the groom heard the news loudly sniffed he,
"The wedding is off I'm too thrifty
  To give my life's care
  To a partner who'll wear
Not one pair of shoes, sir, but fifty."

Ere I finish this tragic recital,
There's a point to explain which is vital,
  The Bride, Fate did balk,
  Was Irish, from Cork,
You'll now see the sense of my title.

This must be one of the best offbeat limericks ever written —

There was an old man of Dunoon,
Who always ate soup with a fork
  For he said "As I eat
  Neither fish, fowl or flesh
I should otherwise finish too quick."

Other limerick books written by Reed included *Sausages and Sundials; The Indiscreet Limerick Book; Limericks for the Beech, Bathroom and Boudoir; Mr Punch's Limerick Book; The New Limerick Book* and many more. Also he was quick to realise that juveniles liked this type of verse, and so wrote books for children, which included *The Child's Own Limerick Book* and *My Limerick Book for Boys and Girls*.

From *Sausages and Sundials* we have this gem —

Consider the lowering Lynx,
He's savage and sullen and stynx,
  Though he never has stunk
  Like the scandalous skunk,
That's a task far beyond him, methinks!

In *The Indiscreet Limerick Book* published in 1928 Reed gave the world a new party game. His idea was to take a gazetteer or timetable — open it at random, and compose limericks using the places named. Here is an example that has stood the test of time —

Said a breeder of goldfish at Wandsworth
"How much are the fish in my ponds worth?"
Said an expert "For fee
I will sort them and see
For a brunette's worth more than a blonde's worth."

To compile *Mr Punch's Limerick Book* published in 1934 Reed collected limericks printed in *Punch* magazine over the years, since it was first published in the mid-nineteenth century. This magazine was a great promoter of the form, and recognised the value of the limerick as an aid to scholars.

Here is an excerpt from *Punch* published in 1904 —

> *The value of the limerick as a handmaiden to history has not been sufficiently considered by the commentators who have ministered to its revival. Many of the smaller and significant phases of modern life can find adequate record in its irresponsible jocundity. Other chroniclers jumble, hesitate, doubt, and stammer; the limerick goes straight to the point touching the events of the moment.*

For example this verse was composed by Professor Harvey Carter, at Colorado College, USA to help students remember the value of pi —

'Tis a favourite project of mine
A new value of pi to assign;
I would fix it at 3
For it's simpler, you see,
Than 3 point 14159.

This one entitled 'Relativity' was published in *Punch* in the early 1920s and was written by Professor Arthur Buller, a world authority on fungi —

There was a young lady named Bright
Whose speed was faster than light;
She went out one day
In a relative way,
And returned the previous night.

To her friends said the Bright one in chatter
"I have learnt something new about matter;
My speed was so great
Much increased was my weight
Yet I failed to become any fatter!"

In many of his limerick books Reed attempted to classify the verses he presented. For example, he had sections on classical verse, sports, stock exchange, the seaside, and many others.

The clerical profession have been loyal instigators of the form from early days, and Reed collected many anonymous verses written by clerics or about them.

Here is a selection as presented by Reed in his earlier limerick books —

There was a young monk of Siberia,
Who of fasting grew wearier and wearier,
  Till at length with a yell,
  He burst from his cell,
And devoured the Father Superior.

There were two ladies of Birmingham,
I know a sad story concerning 'em.
  They stuck needles and pins
  In the right reverend's shins,
Of the Bishop engaged in confirming 'em.

There was an old person of Fratton,
Who would go to Church with his hat on.
  "If I wake up" he said
  "With my hat on my head,
I shall know that it hasn't been sat on."

There was an Archdeacon of Bristol
Who murdered his niece with a pistol;
  Said he: "I can't bear
  Your absurdly cropped hair,
And your listening in with a crystal."

There was a young tenor of Tring,
Whose nickname was "God Save the King"
  For the kindliest hearted
  Of people departed
Whenever he started to sing.

There was an old prelate of Brittany
Who always went wrong in the Litany
  Exclaimed he: "I can't
  Find a suitable chant,
The words somehow don't seem to fit any."

There was once a pious young priest
Who lived almost wholly on yeast,
"For" he said "it is plain
We must all rise again,
And I want to get started at least."

In the sports section Reed included many verses about cricket. The first refers to W. G. Grace, and is moulded on one of Lear's most famous stanzas —

There was an old man with a beard,
Who said, "I should never have feared
That greyhounds would race
In this sanctified place,"
And every good cricketer cheered.

Here are two verses written by E. C. Holt, about the Surrey cricket team of 1920, and published in Punch, the same year.

When people try googlies on Sandham
You can see he will soon understand 'em.
With a laugh at their slows
He will murmur "Here goes,"
And over the railings will land 'em.

All classes of bowlers have stuck at
Their efforts to dislocate Ducat,
Their wiliest tricks
He dispatches for six,
Which is what they decidedly buck at.

Two more anonymous verses, which cannot be left out!

There was a young man said "Hobbs
Should never be tempted with lobs;
He would knock them about
Till the bowlers gave out,
And watered the pitch with their sobs!"

There's no one as dreadful as Fender
For batsmen whose bodies are tender;
He gets on their nerves
With his murderous swerves,
That insist on death or surrender!

As a tennis player himself, Langford Reed could not ignore this game —

There was a young fellow of Ennis,
Who was very effective at tennis,
  The way he said "Love"
  Made each turtle dove,
Think the racquet more mighty than pen is.

There was a young lady of Venice,
Who used hard boiled eggs to play tennis,
  When they said "Is it wrong?"
  She replied "Go along,
You don't know how prolific my hen is."

Golf was not forgotten —

A young lady whose surname was Binks
Went out for a walk on the Links,
  When a young man cried "Fore"
  She observed "What a bore,
To go home 'foursome' 'tee' when there's drinks."

There was a young golfer of Troon,
Who always played golf with a spoon,
  "It's handy" he said,
  "For the brandy, you see,
Should anyone happen to swoon."

The verses which came under the heading 'Stock Exchange' were very mild!

There was an old fellow of Tyre,
Who constantly sat on the fire,
  When asked "Is it hot?"
  He replied "It is not,
I'm James Winterbottom Esquire."

There was a young lady of Tottenham
Her manners — she'd wholly forgotten 'em.
  While at tea, at the Vicar's
  She took off her mittens
Explaining she felt much too hot in 'em!

There was a young girl of Australia,
Who went to a dance as a dahlia.
  When the petals uncurled
  It revealed to the world,
That the dress as a dress, was a fail–ia!

There was a young lady of Erskine,
Who had a remarkably fair skin,
  When I said to her "Mabel,
  You look well in your sable"
She replied "I look best in my bearskin."

The next verse was sent to Langford Reed after a particularly naughty batch of limericks had been received by a clergyman.

Your verses, dear Fred, I surmise,
Were not meant for clerical eyes,
  The Bishop and Dean
  Cannot think what they mean,
And the curate turns pink with surprise.

Here are three limericks which deal with the subject of the seaside —

There's a place that's called Westcliff–on–Sea
A paradox quite seems to me,
  For its cliffs have "Gone West"
  And as for the rest,
There's mud where the sea ought be.

At Eastbourne —

An old man who sat on the front
Did nothing but gurgle and grunt,
  But those not at hand
  Thought it came from the band,
And encored this original stunt!

Ebenezer and Florence from Bow,
Went out in a small boat to row.
  But before very long...
  Well, the tide was too strong,
Now their friends call the pair Ebb and Flo.

Reed collected limericks which punned the English way of spelling and pronunciation —

There was a young fellow of Gloucester
Whose wife ran away with a coucester,
He traced her to Leicester,
And tried to arreicester,
But in spite of his efforts he loucester.

A girl who weighs many an Oz.
Used language I will not pronoz.
Her brother one day,
Pulled her chair right away,
He wanted to see if she'd boz.

An unpopular youth of Cologne,
With a pain in his stomach did mogne,
He heaved a great sigh
And said "I would digh
But the loss would be only my ogne."

An obstinate lady of Leicester,
Wouldn't marry her swain, though he preicester,
For his income I fear,
Was a hundred a year,
On which he could never have dreicester!

Langford Reed included a fair selection entitled 'Favourites' —

There was a young poet of Kew,
Who failed to emerge into view,
So he said, "I'll dispense,
With rhyme, metre and sense,"
And he did, and he's now in *Who's Who.*

There was a young lady of Eton,
Whose figure had plenty of meat on,
She said "Marry me Jack,
And you'll find that my back
Is a nice place to warm your cold feet on."

There was a young lady from Keithley,
Whose principal charm in her teeth lay,
  When they fell on her plate,
  She called out "I hate
Mishaps of this kind, they are beathly."

There was a young lady of Jarrow,
Whose mouth was exceedingly narrow,
  Though times out of number,
  She chewed a cucumber,
She never could manage a marrow.

There was an old hag of Malacca,
Who smoked such atrocious tobacca,
  When tigers came near,
  They trembled with fear,
And did not attempt to attack her.

There was a young woman of Thrace,
Whose nose spread all over her face.
  She had very few kisses;
  The reason for this is,
There wasn't a suitable place.

There was a young woman of Ealing
Who thought her friends very unfeeling
  When she had scarlet fever,
  They wouldn't receive her,
So she called on them when she was peeling.

A barber who lived in Batavia,
Was well known for his fearless behaviour,
  An enormous baboon
  Broke in his saloon,
But he murmured "I'm blowed if I'll shavia."

There was an old man of the Nore,
The same shape behind as before,
  They didn't know where,
  To offer a chair,
So he had to sit down on the floor.

There was an old maid of Vancouver,
Who captured a man by manoeuvre,
For she jumped on his knee,
With a chortle of glee,
And nothing on earth could remove her.

A thoughtful old man of Lanore,
When a subject was getting a bore,
Would wisely arrange,
Conversation to change,
By falling in fits on the floor.

A traveller once to his sorrow,
Desired to take tickets to Morro,
But they said "Go away,
You can't book today
For a journey you're taking tomorrow."

A maiden at college named Breeze,
Weighed down by BAs and MDs.
Collapsed from the strain
Said her doctor "It's plain
You are killing yourself by degrees.

There was a young man of Herne Bay
Who was making some fireworks one day,
But he dropped his cigar
In a gun powder jar,
There WAS a young man of Herne Bay.

The education authorities of London and Middlesex employed Langford Reed to give lectures on literary subjects to schools and colleges. He also was in much demand to give talks to societies and clubs. In 1925 he gave a lecture to the English Speaking Union on the subject of 'English and American Limericks'. In his speech he remarked once again on the remarkable talent that the clergy had for this type of verse. He mentioned that some churches had even adopted the limerick metre to be used in the instruction of the catechism because it was popular and easy to remember!

He reported that the famous societies of St Peter and St Paul were working on similar lines in both England and America, and had just published a limerick prayer book, the preface of which went like this —

These rhymes were designed by a priest,
To affect your religion like yeast,
  If they help it to grow
  Like the yeast in the dough
There'll be one better Christian at least!

Mr Reed also quoted one of the limericks made famous by Dean Inge, often called 'the gloomy Dean' —although his limericks belie his description!

We thought him an absolute lamb,
But when he sat down in the jam
  On taking his seat
  At our Sunday school treat,
We all heard our Vicar say — "Stand up while I say grace."

Langford Reed was an industrious and prolific writer and produced many more books on literary subjects. He was a passionate devotee of Lewis Carroll and wrote *The Life and Works of Lewis Carroll* published in 1934. Other works included *Anthology of Nonsense Verse; Stories of Charlie Chaplin Films* and *Daphne Grows Down* in collaboration with his wife, Hetty Spiers. He wrote the scenarios for many films, and frequently broadcast from his own works. He also wrote *The Prime Minister's Pyjamas; The Complete Rhyming Dictionary* and *The King of the Jesters.*

When the Second World War broke out, Reed enlisted as an RAF officer in 1940, by knocking a few years off his age. When he was found out he said "I am not responsible for my birth certificate — I was only a tiny baby when it was made out!" He was allowed to stay.

After the war he continued writing and although his health deteriorated, this did not affect his output. He was helped considerably in the last years of his life by his daughter Joan, to whom he dictated his works after his arm had become paralysed. And ill health never changed his humorous outlook on life. He even contemplated death with a smile —

Here is the ending to a poem about his three dogs —

With these three comrades true, I hope to be,
When I have shuffled off this coil called mortal,
But if when I arrive these words I see,
Upon a placard on the outer portal —
"No dogs admitted" — I shall know full well
That I have missed my road and come to…!

Herbert Langford Reed was writing a play and a new book of poems, when in 1954, he died.

Although saddened by her father's death, Miss Joan Langford Reed said — "We feel happier because he left so much laughter in the world behind him. His idea of heaven was a place where there was work to be done."

In some ways, Edward Lear and Herbert Langford Reed had similar qualities of personality and character. Both were industrious, working most of their lives at the creative activities that pleased them most. They did not aspire to riches and were content to accept the remuneration from their labours. Each had an extraordinary sense of humour and took pleasure out of simple things, and neither was a lover of convention. And of course both were outstanding limerick men.

In the chapter dealing with the life of Edward Lear, I mentioned that his life's ambition was to be remembered as a landscape artist. But it is for his nonsense verses that Lear is remembered today.

Langford Reed also had a secret ambition — Trevor Bailey told me — to write a best selling novel. He described his uncle as a "great manipulator of words rather than a great teller of tales." But of all his labours it is for his work in the limerick field that earned him the description of the limerick's only historian.

Perhaps Reed's life work can be best described in his own words — entitled 'L'Envoi' —

My pen I can herewith discard
If you study my counsel quite hard,
  You may I forsee,
  A limerick bard be,
And have no more limericks barred.

I said earlier that it must have been very pleasant to know Mr Lear. I am now equally sure that it would have been very pleasant to know Mr Langford Reed also.

8

More Recently

After the cleansing and revival of the limerick by Langford Reed a few contemporary writers in Britain continued to produce the verse form.

Here is an ingenious double limerick written by Walter de la Mare entitled 'Moonshine' — as presented in the Fireside Book of Humorous Poetry edited by William Cole —

There was a young lady of Rheims,
There was an old poet of Gizeh,
He rhymed on the deepest and sweetest of themes.
She scorned all his efforts to please her,
And he sighed "Ah, I see,
She and sense won't agree."
So he scribbled her moonshine and moonshine, and she
With jubilant screams, packed her trunk up in Rheims,
Cried aloud "I am coming O Bard of my dreams."
And was clasped to his bosom in Gizeh.

Most of the more recent British writers of humorous verse cater for children's entertainment. Here is a limerick poem written by William Jay Smith entitled 'Dragon'. It can be found in *Verse That is Fun*, compiled by Barbara Ireson.

A dragon named Ernest Balfour,
Who lived in a dark palace tower,
  Played a dark violin
  Of dried out sharkskin
Hour after hour after hour.

An Indian princess one day,
Who happened to wander that way,
  Said: "The sound of that thin
  Dried out violin
Has stolen my heart away."

So she climbed the steps of the tower,
And there beheld Ernest Balfour,
  Who was changed by her glance
  To a handsome young prince;
She had broken the Old Witch's power.

They were married the very next minute,
By a neighbour, Sir Larchmont of Linnet,
  And they danced to a thin
  Dried out violin
Accompanied by a very shrill spinet.

And Ernest said: "Princess my dear,
I will never blow smoke in your ear,
  No Dragon am I
  But a Prince till I die;
You have nothing whatever to fear.

Let me buy you some angelfood cake
That we'll munch while we walk by the lake,
  Enjoying the smile,
  Of the sweet crocodile
And the music the Bullfrogs make.

When a dragon roars down from the hill,
Having come to do us both ill,
  Belching up flames,
  And calling us names,
I will say GO AWAY! And he will."

The popular comedian Spike Milligan also tried his hand at composing nonsense verse. In his book *Silly Verse for Kids* published by Dobson, he presented these limerick stanzas —

There was a young soldier called Edser,
When wanted was always in bed sir;
  One morning at one,
  They fired the gun
And Edser, in bed sir, was dead sir!

In the land of the Bumbley Boo
The people are red white and blue,
  They never blow noses,
  Or ever wear closes,
What a sensible thing to do!

In the land of the Bumbley Boo
You can buy lemon pie at the Zoo;
  They give away Foxes
  In little Pink Boxes
And bottles of Dandylion Stew.

In the land of the Bumbley Boo
You never see a Gnu,
  But thousands of cats
  Wearing trousers and hats
Made of Pumpkins and Pelican Glue!

Chorus

Oh! the Bumbley Boo! the Bumbley Boo!
That's the place for me and you!
So hurry. Let's run!
The train leaves at one!
For the land of the Bumbley Boo!
The Wonderful Bumbley Boo–Boo–Boo!
The Wonderful Bumbley Boo!!!

Miss Ida Thurtle who wrote under the name of 'Liza Jane', composed limericks for amusement. She specialised in Norfolk and Suffolk place names, especially those with unusual spellings or pronunciations — and there are plenty of those in the East of England!

In her booklet entitled *Let's Laugh a Little*, published by Stockwell, she presented sixty-two limericks with an East Anglian flavour. Miss Thurtle told me that she had been confined to her house for some years with arthritis, and found limerick making an excellent way of passing the time.

Here is a selection of verses from her book —

A poor fellow living at Costessey,
Had a wife who was terrible bostessey,
  "If you're late home" she said,
  With a toss of the head,
"I shall know you've been flirting with Flostessie."

A flighty young lady from Loddon
Fell into a pond and got sodden.
  She took off her clothes,
  And she powdered her nose,
And walked home feeling thoroughly modern.

Said a boy to his brother at Lynn,
"Watch your step when Ma asks where you've bin,
  You might git a hug,
  Or a lip er the lug, [A box on the ear]
Depending in what mood she's in."

A certain young man from Hilgay,
Took his harp to a concert one day;
The audience cheered when on stage he appeared,
But they groaned when he started to play.

A young man who lived at Holme Hale
Went to Acle one day to the sale;
  He waved to his mate,
  And discovered too late,
That he'd purchased five acres of kale.

A curate who worked in Ipswich
Went to church, a young couple to hitch,
"Before I begin" he said with a grin,
"I must really inquire which is which?"

A scatter brained couple at Gissing
Arranged for an afternoon christening;
When they got there she said —
"Where's the baby, then Fred?"
He replied "I thought something was missing."

It has always been said at Upgate
That the profit from mustard is great.
It's not what you eat with your cheese or your meat,
But what's left behind on the plate.

A retired Civil Servant at Gateley,
Who lived in a home known as stately,
Kept lions for fun in a wire-netting run,
But he hasn't been seen around lately.

Said a wife to her husband at Scole
Who'd forgotten to order the coal,
"I knew you'd forget, you've a head like a net;
Where there isn't a knot there's a hole."

A young boxer living in Outwell
Always managed to get through a bout well.
He was light on his toes, good at parrying blows,
And could upper cut, side step, and clout well.

Moaned a broker who lived at Upwell,
"At this game I shall never excel.
Shares are always sky-high when I'm wanting to buy,
And low when I'm trying to sell."

The most prolific and dedicated writer of limericks this side of the Atlantic, in recent years, must surely be author Tony Butler of Co. Dublin, Ireland. True to Irish tradition he has a flair for composing this metrical form, and his book *Best Irish Limericks*, published by Wolfe, proved to be very entertaining.

Here are the six from that publication —

A lady who lived at Newbliss,
Would stand on her head for a kiss,
  When people asked why,
  She replied cute and sly,
"Men go to my head when like this."

As played by the phantoms of Shrule,
Midnight football is eerie and crule,
  If one kicks a ghost
  Past the other's goal post,
He wins credit for scaring a ghoul.

Said a silly old boyo of Sneem,
"My telly is powered by hot steam.
The reception is vile,
But when brought to the bile,
It gives tea — if not V — that's a dream."

A romantic motorist from Ballon,
Called Socrates Oscar O'Fallon,
Is changing his dears,
More oft with the years,
And he's getting twelve girls to the gallon.

A crazy young lad out of Slane,
Had some odd sort of thoughts on his brain.
He swam the rivers of France,
Led the gendarmes a dance,
And though guilty they found him in Seine.

A virile young boyo of Youghal,
Was renowned for his loud mating coughal,
The sound of his voice
Made women rejoice,
In Kilbeggan, Athlone, Sligo, East Hampstead, Duluth,
Kells, Ontario, Tokyo, Ballydehob, Washington, Little
Neck, Cahirciveen, Galway, and of course, St Poughal.

Contemporary writers use this verse form much more frequently than do British authors. Perhaps this is because adult humorous verse is generally much more popular in America than in Britain. In this country it seems to be confined almost entirely to children's literature.

Professor Morris Bishop was champion of the limerick in America for many years. Here is a special contribution entitled 'Sonnet and Limerick' — as published in *Fireside Book of Humorous Poetry.*

The sonnet with her Mona Lisa smile
Broods on the world while others stare.
Priestess of Melancholy darkly fair,
Serene above our fury, guilt and guile,
She in her deeps, has learned to reconcile,
Life's contradictions. Really I declare,
I'd gladly trust a sonnet anywhere,
That pure, seraphic sedentary. While

The limerick's furtive and mean;
You must keep her in close quarantine,
  Or she sneaks to the slums,
  And promptly becomes
Disorderly, drunk and obscene.

Another classic from his book entitled *Spilt Milk*, is this —

There's a tiresome young man from Bay Shore
When his fianceé cried "I adore
  The beautiful sea!"
  He replied "I agree,
It's pretty. But what is it for?"

Conrad Aitken was a prolific writer with a 'soft spot' for comic verse. Here is his summary of the limerick as he saw it, taken from his book *A Seizure of Limericks* —

The limerick's admitted, a verse form;
A terse form; a curse form; a hearse form.
  It may not be lyric
  And at best it's Satyric,
And a whale of a tail in perverse form.

He also wrote offbeats —

LIMBERICK

It's time to make love, Douse the glim
The fireflies twinkle and dim.
  The stars lean together
  Like birds of a feather,
And the lion lies down with the limb.

Ogden Nash must be regarded as one of the most famous writers of humorous verse. And his limericks epitomised his great sense of fun. Here is one called 'Arthur', for no apparent reason!

There was an old man of Calcutta,
Who coated his tonsils with butta,
  Thus converting his snore
  From a thunderous roar,
To a soft oleaginous mutta.

Since Lear there have been many "Old Men of Calcutta" rhymes, but none funnier than this, I think.

Here is a selection of limericks from one of Ogden Nash's more recent books, entitled *There's Always Another Windmill*, published by Andre Deutsch. The limerick section is headed, 'How Pleasant to Ape Mr Lear'.

There once was an umpire whose vision
Was cause for abuse and derision,
  He remarked in surprise,
  Why pick on my eyes?
It's heart that dictates my decision.

A handsome young rodent named Gratian,
As a life guard became a sensation.
  All the lady mice waved
  And screamed to be saved
By his mouse-to-mouse resuscitation.

A crusader's wife slipped from the garrison
And had an affair with a Saracen.
  She was not oversexed,
  Or jealous or vexed,
She just wanted to make a comparison.

A novelist of the absurd
Has a voice that will shortly be heard.
  I learn from my spies
  He's about to devise
An unprintable three letter word.

A lama of Outer Mongolia
Was seized with acute melancholia,
  When the Chinese asked why
  He could only reply
You'd chop off my head if I tolia.

There was a young girl of Milwaukee
Whose voice was sc-reechy and squawky,
  Her friends were emphatic
  She sounded like static
And called her their Milwaukee-talkie.

A few of the modern anonymous limericks taken from the oral collection, are too good to be ignored —

The bottle of perfume Willie sent
Was highly displeasing to Millicent.
  Her thanks were so cold
  That they quarrelled, I'm told,
Through that silly scent Willie sent Millicent.

A flea and a fly in a flue,
Were imprisoned so what could they do?
  Said the fly "Let us flee."
  Said the flea, "Let us fly."
So they flew through a flaw in the flue.

An opera star named Maria
Always tried to sing higher and higher,
  Till she hit a high note
  Which got stuck in her throat —
Then she entered the Heavenly Choir.

There once was a boy of Bagdad
An inquisitive sort of a lad.
  He said, "I will see
  If a sting has a bee."
And very soon he found that it had.

There was a young fellow of Perth
Who was born on the day of his birth.
  He was married they say
  On his wife's wedding day,
And he died when he quitted the earth.

There was a young lady of Rhyl,
Whose general knowledge was nil
  For she thought Joan of Arc,
  Navigated the bark
That landed on Ararat's hill.

There was a young lady of Spain
Who couldn't go out in the rain.
  For she'd lent her umbrella,
  To Queen Isabella,
Who never returned it again.

Winter is here with his grouch,
The time when you sneeze and you slouch;
  You can't take your women
  Canoeing or swimming,
But a lot can be done on a couch.

Have you heard of the knock-kneed Sam Guzzum,
And Samantha his bow-legged cousin?
  "It's true" people say,
  "That love finds a way,"
But for Sam and Samantha it doesn't.

A sleeper from the Amazon
Put nighties of his gra'mazon,
  The reason that,
  He was too fat,
To get his own pajamazon.

An amorous lady antique
Locked a man in her house for a week;
  He entered her door
  With a shout and a roar,
But his exit was marked by a squeak.

On a maiden a man once begat,
Bouncing triplets, named Nat, Tat and Pat,
  'Twas fun in the breeding,
  But hell in the feeding
She hadn't a spare tit for Tat.

There was a co-ed of Cayenne,
Who ate onions, blue cheese, and sen-sen;
  Till a bad fright one day,
  Took her breath right away,
And we hope that she won't find it again.

There was a young lady named Etta,
Who fancied herself in a sweater;
  Three reasons she had
  To keep warm was not bad,
But the other two reasons were better.

Finally here is a poem composed limerick style — the author is unknown, entitled 'The Music that Counts'.

There was a composer named Bong,
Who composed a new popular song:
  It was simply the croon
  Of a lovesick baboon,
With occasional thumps on the gong.

It was slated by Allan (Sir Hugh)
As a "horrible hullabaloo,"
  But it gained many scores
  Of ecstatic encores
In a great super-Tarzan revue.

Moreover, the eminent Bong
Came out in the Press very strong
  When he challenged his foes,
  If they could compose
A more thoroughly popular song.

As for me I felt all along
That both of the parties are wrong;
  I don't care for croons
  Of lovesick baboons
But I love to play tunes on the gong.

9

WINNERS AND RUNNERS

SINCE the great Limerick Era, limerick competitions waxed plentiful in the twentieth century. To the general public, composing a verse worthy of winning a prize was a challenge that few could resist.

The winner in an impromptu contest held in New York in 1925, was Berton Braley. Here is his effort —

There was an old fellow named Bryan
Whose voice was forever cryin'
  Do you think that my shape
  Was derived from an ape?
Well, I think Charlie Darwin was lyin'.

W. S. Baring-Gould's admirable book, *The Lure of the Limerick*, tells of two other American competitions.

During the last war the Mark Twain Society held a competition for the best verse to immortalise their patron. It was won by W. S. Burgess of Nebraska with this clever stanza —

Mark Twain was a mop headed male
Whose narratives sparkled like ale;
  And this Prince of the Grin
  Who once feathered Huck Finn
Can still hold the world by the tale!

And in 1965 a very successful contest was run by a magazine called *Business Week*, in New York. It gave the last line as 'It isn't how many, it's who.' and called for four appropriate lines to precede it. Over 4,000 limericks were submitted and the winner was Alexander G. Ross with this —

If it's management men you pursue,
Don't hunt every beast in the Zoo —
Just look for the signs
That say "Tigers and Lions" —
It isn't how many, it's who.

The first prize was a fortnight in Ireland for two, spending some time in Limerick City, and other places of historical interest, plus 500 dollars spending money, or the cash equivalent of 2,500 dollars. It is interesting to note that owing to the nature of the first prize, perhaps Americans were coming round to thinking that the limerick did originate in Limerick after all.

Nearer home, in April 1970, at Croom, Co. Limerick, a three-day cultural festival, Féile na Máighe (the festival of the Maigue), was sponsored by the Gaelic League, to commemorate the bicentenary of the Maigue Poets.

People flocked in their thousands to attend the celebrations. The small country village of Croom came to life. Tubs of flowers lined the streets. Flags adorned the houses. The sun shone, and the carefree spirit of the Maigue was revived. Happiness mixed with patriotism added flavour to the scene.

The programme included a Court of Poetry, the first to be held for two hundred years in Croom. Two noted Irish poets read verses specially engendered for the occasion. It was rather remarkable that the two men bore identical names as two of the leading Maigue Poets — Séan O'Tuama and Seamus O Cinneide.

Other entertainments were choral speech and singing, concerts, debates and outings. Excursions were made to look at three graves in the area where three of the Maigue Poets were buried. Séan Clárach Mac Dónaill was buried at Ráthluire. Séan O'Tuama (John O'Toumy) in Croom, and Aindrias Mac Craith (Andrew McCrath) in Kilmallock. A monument was unveiled to commemorate Andrew McCrath, and a service of dedication held.

Pre-arranged contests for essays, poetry and limericks were judged. The limerick competition was world wide, and called for entries in English and Gaelic, and there was no censorship.

The contest brought in nearly a thousand entries, and of course, only the printable versions were considered as likely winners!

Dr Robert Wyse Jackson, then Bishop of Limerick, sent in the winning verse, under a pseudonym —

A landlord from Maigueside, O'Toumy,
Hated verses, long winded and gloomy,
On the Limerick he hit,
For its scarifying wit,
In a setting sufficiently roomy.

The Bishop had entered two verses and when on the Saturday night he was told that he had won, he repeated what he thought was the better verse over the Irish Television network. Here is the stanza that was printed in the Sunday papers —

The traditional poets of Maigue,
Knew nothing of White Horse or Haig,
  But uisce beatha hot,
  Distilled in a pot,
Kept them merry, poetic and vague.

However, when the adjudicator was told of this, he hastened to say that it was the Bishop's other entry that had won; but as both were outstanding either could have been successful.

The Bishop wrote under the name of Mac Siacuis (the Gaelic form of Jackson), and by strange coincidence the winner of the Gaelic section was also called by his name — Piaras Mac Siacuis, a school teacher of Co. Limerick. Here is his winning verse —

Tá tailbhse an Tuamaigh mí-shásta
Mar ná fuair sé aon grant ó Bhord Fáilte;
Dá mbeadh ann lena linn,
Mor-dheontas d'á Inn
Nach aige bheadh an roadhouse galánta.

Mr Mac Siacuis (Pearse Jackson) also sent me this translation —

The ghost of O'Toumy's mí-shásta [dissatisfied]
For he got no grant from Bord Fáilte [Irish Tourism organisation]
  Had there been, in his linn [time]
  A large grant for his Inn
Wouldn't he have the Roadhouse galánta. [elegant]

Pearse Jackson explains that a stroke over a vowel in Irish á, í etc., means that the vowel in question is given a long sound — á is aaa, as in 'ward', and ó is ooo, as in 'moor'.

He also explains that his verse as well as referring to John O'Toumy and his pub, also includes the system of the Bord Fáilte–tourist board in Ireland–of giving grants to hoteliers.

Another contest, impromptu this time, was held one evening during the celebrations at Croom. The winning entry was submitted in Irish by a lady called Miss Maire Bhreathnach from Dublin —

Sé dier bruinneal an Icy-Ha-Ha
Go bhfuil mores an phobail as meath
  Go mbionn rudal ró-risqué
  Virginubus puerisqué
Ar síul ins an ait mbiónn Fleádh.

This verse refers to the attitude taken up by the Irish Countrywomen's Association, the Irish equivalent of our Women's Institute, over some misbehaviour during a traditional music festival (a Fleádh Cheovil) some time previously. The author questions that even the Maigue Poets behaved in a disorderly fashion, and were not always sober. 'Icy-Ha-Ha' was her nickname for the Irish Countrywomen's Association.

Here is a translation —

The Icy-Ha-Ha ladies say,
That our morals are all in decay;
  And things much too risqué
  Virginubus puerisqué
Are seen when the Fleádh goes too gay.

Although this verse gained the prize, the sequel is equally good, I think —

"Mo ghreidhin lad" aR Aindrais Mac Craith
Go scoiltfihr mo leac i dhá leath
  Murar bás do ar ndúchas
  La greann is le súbhachas
Le ceol is la hól is le grá!

Translated —

"Not at all" Merry Aindrais replying,
"May my tombstone in fragments be lying
  If it's not brimming glasses
  Love music and lasses,
Make a culture that's living, not dying!"

According to journalists' reports, which were to be found in most Irish, English and American papers the first verse of Maire Bhreathnach's was considered to be the best out of all the winners in this competition.

Quidnunc, who writes in the *Irish Times*, contributed this verse in one of his articles dealing with the festival. Although it was not entered as a runner, I think it sums up the modern concept of the limericks of the Maigues —

There were two old rhymsters from Croom
Who started a literary boom
With a five lined verse,
That was bawdy and terse —
Lim'rick lace, but from no convent loom.

Owing to the outstanding success of the 1970 celebrations, another Croom festival was held in the Spring of 1971. And it was decided to treat the festival as an annual event.

The cultural programme followed the same pattern as its predecessor, and there were of course two limerick contests.

The winner in the English section was Beda Herbert MA. She immortalised part of the Irish history with this stanza entitled 'The Iceberg' —

There was a high cleric named Mannix,
Monumentally cool amid panics;
A fleet he could fool
He played it so cool —
An iceberg among the Titanics.

During the War of Independence in Ireland in the early 1920s the Mannix of the limerick (Daniel Mannix), who was Catholic Archbishop of Melbourne at the time, sailed for his native Ireland to help in the fight for freedom. On nearing the Irish coast, a fleet of British warships intercepted his ship, and he was arrested and brought to England. The British government thought he was too dangerous to be allowed on Irish soil, and he wasn't permitted to land.

The second prize was gained by Joe Roe whose limerick had a distinctly political flavour. 'Teague' (from the Irish Tadhg, Timothy) is the name applied by their opponents to Catholics in Northern Ireland; and Bill Craig was a member of the Northern Ireland Government, and was regarded as a 'hard liner'.

There was a young man from the Maigue,
Gaelic speaker, no doubt, and a Teague;
Has the tongue that he spoke
Almost spoke its last croak,
Now we all share the speech of Bill Craig?

The first prize in the Irish section went to Piaras Mac Siacuis, the same winner as the previous year —

Nach áit í an áit i an Dáil;
Gan ach bradán is scileadh ar fáil
Ach fóill ort go fóill,
Is ann bhéas an ceol
Nuair a bheidh ann an da Fhianna Fáil.

Translated it reads —

A peculiar place is the Dáil [Irish Parliament]
Where TDs only gossip and brawl,
  But, patience awhile
  There'll be music more vile
When they have there the two Fianna Fáils.

Pearse Jackson offered the following explanation —

My 1971 verse comments on our Dáil or House of Commons, where the exchanges between the members are, occasionally, less than charitable, and also refers to the impending split in Fianna Fáil our Government Party.

Two other runners-up worthy of mention in the contest are —

There was a Wyse Bishop named Jackson,
On subjects he had many cracks on;
  With the poets of the Maigue
  He was not at all vague
Though his name was not Gaelic but Saxon
(Henry Lorton)

And —

When O Riada his lecture had given
The chairman expressed an opinion;
  "The butterflies fair
  You lured in from the air,
Sean, I fear you're a man in a million."
(Dónall O Ceocháin)

There is a sad sequel to the last verse. Séan O Raida died the following year at the age of forty. He was a brilliant composer and musician, and lectured in Irish Music at University College, Cork. All Ireland mourned this wonderfully talented man who died at the height of his powers, and of his promise.

He has been described as one of the 'corner stones' of Cumann na Máighe — the group responsible for the origination of the festival called Féile na Máighe, and his place was very difficult to fill.

In a letter to me Dónall O Ceocháin said that the last line of his limerick was undoubtedly true.

In Britain 1971 must be regarded as a Limerick year. To kick off, in January we had the BBC1 programme *Nationwide* sponsoring a last line contest, for which over

5,000 limericks were submitted.

In April, the BBC programme *Look East*, which is affiliated to *Nationwide*, staged a contest for my benefit. The response was tremendous, and entries continued to arrive long after the closing date. People of all ages took part. Many verses were from children, and some of those are featured in the 'Child's Play' section.

Here is the winner, sent in by Miss Ida Thurtle —

There's a boxer residing at Gissing
Who can never say 's' without hissing.
  Of the teeth in his mouth,
  One points north, and one south,
And the rest of the front ones are missing.

Second place was gained by Mrs F. O. Brewster with this —

There was an old lady of Hake,
Who said "I will bake a fine cake;"
  She threw in some stones,
  And a bag of old bones,
Three trowels, two forks, and a rake.

And third in line, was this verse, written by Mrs B. Sutton —

There was a young lady of Lynn,
Who thought it a terrible sin;
  To cover her mini
  With such a long pinny,
She bought a new midi in Lynn.

It has been said that the gentle sex does not like limericks. This surely has been disproved with three lady winners in this section!

Many original verses submitted were too good to be overlooked. Here is a selection of 'winners' in my own mind!

There once was a lady named Anna,
In the choir she sang the soprana,
  The choirmaster said
  As she stood on her head
"Hosanna, you show your hose Anna."
(Lucy Williams)

There was once a fair maid of Penzance,
Who stifled all thoughts of romance,
  But as she grew older,
  And the knights became colder
She wished she had taken her chance.
(J. A. Johnson)

There was once a driver from Calais
While during the Rome-Turin rally,
  Felt his head reel
  And lost grip of the wheel
Chamber music? — I'm in the Po Valley!
(J. M. Hudson, 84 years)

For six hundred years at St Ives
The valiant Old Bridge still survives
  Traffic's battering ram —
  But who cares a dam?
If it crumbles — then so will St Ives!
(Miss M. Tyrell)

During a rainy spell, this verse gained first prize in a WI competition, and was sent in by Miss N. Saunders.

There was a cute fellow named Noah
Who knew when rain came it would pour,
  So he built a nice ark
  But thought it no 'lark'
When the elephant stuck in the door.

This verse was sent in by G. C. Haines, and refers to the unique position of the Bishop's throne in Norwich Cathedral.

Said the Bishop of Norwich: "Perhaps
It's pretentious to sit in the apse,
  But this may atone
  For the site of my throne —
It's swell for controlling the chaps!"

Four ladies from Northwold, Norfolk, engendered some clever safety limericks —

Though this wonderful age has decreed,
We should all charge along at great speed,
  Though we all know we're in it
  Just hold hard a minute,
And then with due caution proceed.

(Miss A. Brunton)

Each morning you're doing your chores,
And busily polishing floors,
  Don't shine under mat
  You might slip and go flat —
And find you had fractured your "jaws."

(Mrs Tooley)

There was a young lad from Northwold
Who was most incredibly bold.
  When he climbed up a pylon,
  He still had a smile on,
It goes well with his halo of gold!

(Mrs R. Crisp)

There was a young man from the City,
The way that he drove was a pity;
  The 30 mile sign
  Was a pretty design
His widow gets all of the kitty.

(Miss C. Carter)

There was an old man from, Llanfairpwllgwyngngyllgogery
chwyrndroowilllantysiliogogoch,
We tried to make it rhyme but we can't.

(Miss Kim Hughes)

Limericks have long been used on the political scene. Surely the oldest example must be the one published in *Punch* in 1845, which alluded to the Reform Bill of 1832, and Lord Brougham who was Lord Chancellor at the time —

There was an old broom of St Stephen's,
That set all at sixes and sevens;
  And to sweep from the room
  The convictions of Brougham,
Was the work of the Broom of St Stephen's.

In July 1971, this verse form was quoted in Parliament by two leading MPs during a debate on the Common Market. Mr Michael Foot reported that there had been a lot of talk sitting on the fence recently, but in the case of the Home Secretary, Mr Maudling, the fence had collapsed! There was much laughter in the House when he added that he was reminded of the limerick —

There was an old bear at the zoo,
Who could always find something to do.
  When it bored him to know
  To walk to and fro,
He reversed it and went fro and to.

Mr Maudling had his own back at the end of the four day debate, he quoted another limerick — alluding to Mr Wilson and his opinion on the Market —

There was a young man of Brent,
Whose foot was unhappily bent,
  To save him the trouble,
  He bent it back double,
And instead of coming, he went.

The House roared with laughter.

The *Daily Mail*, having reported this news with interest, decided to run its own political limerick competition. It was launched in August, and brought forth over 5,000 entries.

The first prize was won by no other than the Rt. Revd Sidney Cyril Bulley, then Bishop of Carlisle, and at one time Chaplain to the Queen. Here is his winning contribution entitled 'The Saga of Harold and Ted' —

"Common Market?" said Harold, "Of course
I'll plead with de Gaulle till I'm hoarse,
  We'll go on a spree —
  Just Georgie and me,
We'll pull off a real tour de force."

"Non, non," said de Gaulle with a shout,
"I'm determined to keep Britain out."
  Harold puffed at his pipe,
  Said "The moment's not ripe,
But the cause is quite right, I've no doubt."

But suddenly Harold was sacked
And strange to relate — though 'tis fact —
  When Ted came along,
  Harold's "right" became "wrong" —
He abandoned the cause he had backed.

"Naughty! Naughty!" said Shirley and Roy,
"Let's restrain this obstreperous boy —
  His hatred of Ted
  Must have gone to his head
Or he would not these tactics employ."

Good George he spoke up like a man
Saying "Ted's terms are the same as our plan,
  He's not a bad bloke
  Who can at a stroke
Wipe the floor with the General's ban."

Harold James leaves the course in a huff,
Edward George sails along through the rough,
  "Ship ahoy! Harold dear
  I'll soon be in the clear
I'm so sorry you've made such a muff."

"But meet me in Brussels, dear man,
For a drink to the EEC plan,
  Bring Jenkins and George,
  New friendships to forge,
You've muffed it, ça ne fait rien."

In my letter to the Bishop I inquired why he thought it was that clerics throughout history have had a special aptitude for this verse form. He replied that he supposed it must be that as words are part of a clergyman's tools in as much as his ministry is concerned with preaching and teaching, he has some way to become a master of words, and frequent public speaking contributes a great measure to this. The Bishop went on to say that his Saga only took forty-five minutes to compose, and was done in great comfort, in bed, to be precise!

He wrote many limericks in his time, to amuse himself and his friends, although he did write more serious verse, also.

I think the fact that two Bishops won major limerick contests in the span of sixteen months, is rather remarkable to say the least!

Here are four verses which gained runner-up prizes.

Our grinning Prime Minister, Heath,
Has beautiful shiny white teeth.
  So they don't tarnish
  He coats them with varnish —
But thometimeth they stick when he eatth.

(Robert Sugden)

I said "Mr Home, I presume?"
He answered in voice full of gloom,
  "Pronounce room like Rome;
  I'm Hume when I'm Home,
And he whom you call Home is Hume."

(Archibald Saunders)

There was a young woman called Devlin
Who thought one or two laws needed'levelin'.
  When asked "Wot no Dad!"
  She replied "Don't look sad,
I'm in a condition I revelin!"

(Jane Dawson)

Said Ted with remarkable candour,
"These limericks are mocking my grandeur,
  So Harold and me
  United we be
And sue everybody for slander."

This verse makes a fitting end to the political limerick competition, and was written by Miss Margot Juby, who was only fifteen years of age at the time.

In August, also, a limerick contest was launched by the *Eastern Evening News*. It called for original rhymes using East Anglian place names.

The response was very gratifying. Here are the prize winners —

First was the verse sent in by S. C. Turner.

A youth and a maiden from Costessey
Sat and talked on a bank that was mostessey;
  After five hours of this
  The youth ventured a kiss...
Not exactly a speed-merchant wastessey?

[Costessey is pronounced 'Cossey'!]

C. K. Thompson who told me that he was only ten years old gained second prize with the following —

There was an old farmer of Watton
Who planted his fields full of cotton,
  But when nothing would grow
  He wanted to know
If the reels he had planted were rotten.

There were so many good runner-up rhymes that they were published at a later date — three with illustrations.

A duzzy ole fule outa Hethersett
Outa-doors in tha inclement weather set,
By the side a the rud
Eatin' cold Christmas pud,
With his top dentures in, but no nether set.
(T. K. Scott)

There was a young lady from Diss
Whose boyfriend asked her for a kiss
She said "You young fool,
Though you do come from Scole
You can't treat a Diss girl like dis."
(H. M. Smith)

There was a young lady from Witton
Whose hot-pants (or so it was written),
Were too small for her bottom,
And as they were cotton
They split, and her bottom was bitten.
(E.R. Franklin)

There was an old woman of Wymondham
Whose dresses were torn, so she pymondham;
  She walked into town
  With her hems hanging down
And the pins scratched her legs and half skymondham.
(Kate Taylor)

There were two gay young people of Trowse
Who were trying to buy a new house.
  But the mortgage man said
  (And they went very red)
"You will first have to make her your spouse!"
(Mrs G. Cartmell)

I once knew a fellow from Thurton
Who pursued every girl with a skirt on,
  When he found one at last
  He cried "Damn and blast!"
For her name was Elizabeth Burton.
(C. F. Simmons)

My favourite neice of Hingham
Was married at church in green gingham;
  She said "Uncle Hubert
  I do love you too, but,
If you don't know the hymns, please don't sing 'em!"
(H. Youngs)

There was a young lady from Gissing
Whose favourite pastime was kissing
  From twilight till dark
  She made hay in the park,
And spent all the night reminiscing.
(Mrs Margaret Clarke)

This verse was sent to me privately by T. K. Scott, and although it did not find a published place in the contest, I feel it worthy of mention, as it uses a place name in every line, and it may be unique in this way —

A harassed young couple from Yaxham
Find their kids, though they Frettenham, tax 'em.
  Till, Home-coming by gad,
  Their by now Seething dad,
One night takes them upstairs and Waxham.

Other verses have been sent to me by enthusiastic limerick writers and I include a selection, the first being 'The Saga of Thorpe School' by Mrs Hale.

There was a young boy from Thorpe School
Who stood on his head on a stool,
  The silly young fat head
  Has now got a flat head
And is two inches shorter, poor fool.

There was a young boy from Thorpe School
Who dived fully clothed in the pool,
  But it wasn't funny
  His blazer was runny,
That crimson young man from Thorpe School.

There was a young boy from Thorpe School
Who had ears on his head like a mule
  But he tuned them to listen
  Not one thing he was missin'
That boy from Thorpe School was no fool.

There was a young boy from Thorpe School
Who pinged pellets of ink with his rule,
  But Oh! such a disaster
  He was caught by the master
And got six of the best after school!

Here are two by Mrs Margaret Clarke who said she made them up in the bath!

There was a young lady from Dereham
The boys wouldn't let her go near 'em.
  She said "Have I B.O.?"
  They said "Dear me No!
It's your fags luv, you know we can't bear 'em."
[Dereham is pronounced Dear-am]

There was a young lady from Beccles
Who hated the sight of her freckles
  Her mother said "Dear
  You need have no fear
Men love them, they're only sun speckles."

Mrs G. Cartmell wrote this one —

There was a young bank clerk of Fakenham,
Who at bank notes was clever at fakin' 'em.
  But he did one too many
  And now hasn't any,
To prison the coppers have taken 'im.

Miss Beda Herbert, now married to Liam Brophy, was the 1971 winner of the Irish competition, as seen earlier. She sent me two more limericks which were great favourites in her family —

There was an old man of Antigua,
Whose wife said to him, "What a pig you are!"
  He answered "My Queen
  Is it manners you mean
Or do you refer to my figua?"

There was a young man from the Cam
Went in for his final exam.
  When he asked if he'd passed
  And they said "No, you're last,"
He turned on his heel and said "Gentleman you surprise me!"

Liam Brophy has caught the limerick urge, and submitted this clever stanza —

There is a young scholar of Ennis,
Whose very particular yen is
  To prove, spite his name,
  Old Kierkergaard's claim
To a life philosophia perennis.
[Kierkergaard means churchyard]

Finally another verse from Ireland by Dónall O Ceocháin —

A blackbird, a thrush, and a starling,
Had a song contest one morning.
  The judge was a crow,
  The result you will know,
When someone discovers what "caw" means.

10
Child's Play

WHETHER we like it or not probably our first knowledge of the limerick verse was gleaned in the schoolroom. Things have not changed. Together with the other poetry metres, the limerick is still a part of the curriculum. Unlike other verse patterns it is immediately recognised by children as one of the highlights of the English lesson. Here at least is something to smile at — something to laugh at. Teacher and child alike can relax and enjoy the metrical swing and humorous results.

Lear's verses are studied and appreciated. Most children find them funny. Most adults think they are childish and tame. The taste for fun, like so many other things, has changed considerably over the years.

Children's humour often leaves adults cold. Adult's humour often leaves children frozen! But I think you will agree that the contributions as presented in this section appeal to most age groups.

Here is a selection of limericks written by children and published as weekly prize winners in the comic called *Sparky*.

A short sighted Russian called Bakeski,
One day made a dreadful mistakeski,
He thought a brown bear
(Fast asleep) was a chair,
He discovered his mistakeski too lateski!

(Patricia Merrien)

There was a young man called McVittie,
Who played football for Birmingham City —
He scored ninety goals
Each one with his nose.
Now it's all flat — what a pity!

(Lesley Minchella)

A foolish old farmer called Brow,
Gummed feathers all over a cow.
  He said, "Go and sing,
  You stupid great thing!
Don't you know you're a dicky-bird now?"
(Edward O'Neil)

There was a young man of Belfast,
Who ran in a race and came last,
  He said "That's enough!
  I'm all out of puff!"
As a tortoise came thundering past.
(Carl Stevenson)

A cheerful young convict called Dahlia
Said, "Diggin' your way out can't fail ya!"
  He dug for a week
  Then gave a great shriek
When he came out in Sydney, Australia!
(Elizabeth Dowall)

A swimmer who swims in Loch Ness
Admits that she wants to confess.
  "The monster's a hoax,
  Just listen here, folks,
It's ME with my hair in a mess!"
(Elizabeth Murdoch)

There was a young man from Calcutta,
Who wanted to sleep in a shutter.
  I'm sorry to say
  The shutter gave way,
And he had to make do with the gutter.
(Nicholas Helson)

There was a young lady named Hannah,
Who was caught in a flood at Montana.
  She floated away,
  And her sister, they say,
Accompanied her on the piano.
(Anthony Concannon)

In the limerick contest held by BBC1's television programme *Look East*, as dealt with earlier, a good selection of verses were sent in by children. Although they did not gain prizes, I think they are worthy of mention — and each one was metrically perfect.

This one refers to man's recent attempts to fly with man-made wings —

The birdman of Peterborough,
Was not particularly thorough,
His wings were too thin
So he nosed dived in,
And the birds sang "There goes another."
(Jonathan White, aged 11)

There is a bandy-legged policeman from Crewe,
Who doesn't know *what* to do.
He can stop without fuss,
A lorry or bus,
But bubble cars simply go through!
(Ceri Hughes, aged 15)

There was a young lad from Cheddar,
Whose face grew redder and redder,
After he'd been told
That he'd just sold
Best Stilton to Lord Tedder.
(Georgina Bell, aged 12)

Here is a verse from our youngest contributor —

There was a young lady from Bute,
Who played on a silver gilt flute,
She played several jigs
To her uncle's white pigs,
That amusing young lady of Bute.
(Claire Porter, aged 7)

There was an old man from Biggles,
Who was always getting the giggles.
His wife said "John
You're putting them on,
As no one in Biggles gets giggles."
(Josephine McDonagh, aged 9)

There was a young boy called Nicky
Who always went round very sticky,
  His mother said "Wash"
  He replied "I'm not posh,"
That cheeky young boy called Nicky.

And —

There was a poor man of Costessey,
Whose beard turned suddenly mossy,
  He exclaimed one day
  "Haven't I turned grey?"
Thus saith the poor man of Costessey.
(Catherine Clinton, aged 12)

A competition was staged recently at Thorpe St Andrew School, Norwich, and over a hundred limericks were submitted. It was a difficult task to pick prize winners, as the standard was high. Here are the three finally decided on —

First — written by Christine Cogman, aged 11.

There was once a very small fox,
Who used to live in a box,
  One night very late,
  He stood near a gate
And there he caught chicken pox.

Second prize was awarded to Andrew George, aged 13.

There was a young fellow from Stoke,
Who told such a terrible joke,
  It got people so bored,
  He was posted abroad,
Where he relates it to French foreign folk.

And the third went to Jason Hall, aged 11.

There was a young man from Australia,
Who painted himself like a dahlia,
  The colours were bright,
  And the sun was just right
But the scent was a perfect failure.

These were too good to miss!

There once was a man called Husein
Who died in agonising pain.
  The gun went CRACK!
  He was shot in the back
And never was seen again.
(Richard Noble, aged 11)

There was a young lady from Lop
Who drank a bottle of pop,
  She drank it so quick
  Every sip, every lick
And swallowed the bottle and top!
(Julie Ling, aged 14)

There was a young girl from New Guinea
Who loved to wear a short mini,
  When the boys sung and cheered
  Round the bend she disappeared
What a queer young girl from New Guinea.
(Sandra Larter, aged 13)

There was an old man from Clutter,
Who had a mysterious stutter,
  He fell out of bed,
  And all that he said,
Was curse my nu- nu- nu- nutter!
(Kim Broom, aged 12)

There was an old woman from Leeds,
Who swallowed a packet of seeds,
  The year after next,
  A branch like a flex
Came growing right out of her knees!
(Deborah Page, aged 13)

There was a young man from Pool
Who was always acting the fool,
  He tried very hard
  To remain on his guard,
But ended up anxious and cruel.
(Glynis Coombes, aged 13)

There was an old man of Ghent,
Who used to sleep in a tent,
  The tent was so small,
  He could not sleep at all
And he forgot what the word sleep meant.
(Hazel Dunn, aged 13)

There was once a man from North Walsham
Who took out his teeth to wash 'em.
  His wife said "Jack
  If you don't put 'em back
I'll tread on the things and squash 'em.
(John Heard, aged 11)

There was a young lady named Ida,
Who could drink nothing but cider,
  One day for a spree
  She drank some coff-ee
Which she found on the table beside her.
(Colin Emms, aged 13)

There was an old woman from Lurkin,
Who loved to eat pickled gurkins
  One day for tea,
  She ate thirty-three,
And pickled her internal workings.
(Jason Penny, aged 12)

There was a young man from York,
Whose budgie began to squawk,
  So he said with a grin,
  As he pushed his beak in,
"I only like budgies that talk."
(Malcolm Farrow, aged 12)

There was an old man called Rus,
Who was knocked down by a bus,
  When asked "Are you dead?"
  He nodded his head,
And caused quite a bit of a fuss.
(Pamela Murphy, aged 13)

There was a footballer called Best,
Who to the other team was a pest,
With his speed with the ball
He dribbled them all,
While the other ten men had a rest!
(David Harrowven, aged 13)

There was a young man from Dublin
Who had a baby pet goblin,
As it grew up,
It fell in a cup,
And came out a limpin' and hoblin'.
(Susan Meazey, aged 12)

There was a young lady called Jean
Who was always so horrid and mean,
One day she awoke
And found it a joke,
To be kind, always willing and keen!
(Diane Oakley, aged 12)

There was a young lady called Sue,
Who was at the end of a queue,
So she said to her friend
"I'll go round the bend
If I don't get in front of this queue."
(Jean Barber, aged 12)

There was a young man from Leicester,
Who had a great hairy chester,
The hairs they were brown
And it made people frown,
On the silly young man from Leicester.
(Henry Crick, aged 13)

There was a young boy from Thorpe School,
Who fell in a ginormous whirlpool!
He span round and round,
And then he found,
He wasn't a boy from Thorpe School.
(Richard Hale, aged 11)

There was a young lady from Rome,
Who thought she would like to leave home.
  The more miles she covered
  The more she discovered,
There's no place on Earth quite like home.
(Julie Swatman, aged 11)

THE ASTRONAUT

An Astronaut went to the moon,
He said he would be back quite soon,
  In this he was wrong
  He was there very long.
He never came back from the moon.
(B. Shrubrook, aged 12)

There was a young lady from Morse,
Who was always found riding a horse,
  While riding she bounced
  She floated and flounced
And ended up in some green gorse.
(Clare Waldon, aged 12)

There was a young man named Flin,
Who swallowed a bottle of gin,
  He was shook up and down
  Till his trousers fell down,
And was promptly rechristened young sin.
(Janette Walker, aged 12)

Towards the end of 1971 the children's television programme *Blue Peter*, staged yet another limerick contest — for children this time. The best contributions were to be published later, in the *Blue Peter Limerick Book*.

The response was very good, and the standard surprisingly high.

Composing limericks is a pastime which finds favour with the younger generation. Other lessons may fade in the memory but limerick making is not so easily forgotten. The future of the limerick verse looks secure.

11
The Entertainers

In the Limerick boom at the turn of the last century, many famous people wrote limericks which have been recorded. Others, less famous, have achieved immortality because of their verses.

It occurred to me that it might be worth while to find out whether the well known personalities of recent years are as interested in limericks as their predecessors. As this verse form is essentially humorous I directed my queries to top comedians and entertainers in the busy world of show business. I wrote to many artistes, and was delighted with the response.

I think you will agree that this modern, star-studded collection well balances the esteemed contributions of many years ago.

These laughter-makers are limerick-makers also, and their special verses make a fitting finale to this book.

Benny Hill was regarded as one of the funniest men in the business, and needs no introduction. He kicked off with this contribution —

A dashing young lady named Hood
Wore a bathing suit made out of wood;
But the sun was too hot
It burnt the darn lot,
I was there, jolly good, jolly good!

That all round entertainer Arthur Askey sent me this original —

A lovely young lady named Kate
Said "The leak in my bath, it can't wait."
Came the plumber next minute
While she was still in it,
Now she's a cute plumber's mate.

Leslie Crowther was very popular both on stage and television. He found time to compose these two limericks —

A Lancashire Lassie named Nance,
Said "With fellers I don't stand a chance;
Not one of them flirts
When I wear Mini-skirts,
I'll have to try wearing Hot-Pance!"

Said a teacher with some indignation
"I hate films on Sex Education
I feel such a fool
When I show them in school —
Now they're asking for 'Birth of the Nation'!"

Comedian and musician Ted Ray, sent me this clever original —

A comedy fiddler named Ray
In an orchestra started to play,
But a rival, 'tis said,
Struck poor Ted on the Head,
And he died in a 'VIOLINT' Way.

Cardew Robinson offered some limericks from his repertoire. He obviously liked the verse form, and chose four favourites, which he thought were suitably clean but still funny!

There was a young man of Milan
Who wrote verses that never would scan;
When his friends asked him why
He would always reply —
"I like to get as many words into the last line as I possibly can!"

There was a young girl named Hilda
Who was madly desired by a builder,
He said that he would,
And he should, and he could
And he did, and he ruddy near killed her!

An unfortunate girl from Torbay
On a slow boat to China, one day,
  Was trapped near the tiller
  By a sex mad gorilla,
And China's an awfully long way!

This one he described as 'silly' —

There was a young man from Torquay
Who was stung on the neck by a wasp;
  When they replied "Does it hurt?"
  He replied "Yes it does!
I'm so glad it wasn't a hornet!"

John le Mesurier was a versatile and polished actor, and was equally at home with comedy and drama. He wrote the following —

There was a young man from Bombay
Who fell into the sea, one day;
  But when he got out
  He exclaimed with a shout,
"I'm not black, just a pale shade of grey!"

The relaxed style and kindly humour of Max Bygraves has earned him a special niche in the hearts of the British public. Here is his own special verse —

A lady I know from Norwich
Is kinky about lumpy porridge,
  She will go to a fete
  And then order a plate,
And that takes a great deal of corridge.

Eric Sykes, who also writes much of his own material, took just five minutes to compose this gem —

"Tell me Tiger," said Isobel Stranks,
"Have you always had stripes on your flanks?"
  The Tiger said, "No
  I'm ambitious and so
I just worked my way up from the ranks."

That master of farce Brian Rix, who wrote most of the material for his plays, was the instigator of the verse quoted in *Simple Spymen*. He proffered the following lines —

There was a young lady from Leeds
Who swallowed a packet of seeds
  And the blades of grass
  Grew out of her —
And her chest was covered in weeds!

Spike Milligan, as well as being a top comedian, wrote scripts and books of humorous verse — as we have seen earlier.

He was especially interested in limericks, and sent the following to include in this section —

A man called Carrington Bride,
Cared not if he lived or he died.
  But when he was dead
  He lay on his bed,
And he cried and he cried, and he cried.

Here is Wilfred Pickles' favourite limerick —

Said the gloomy Dean of St Paul's
As he gazed at the crumbling walls,
  "Do you think it will do
  If we fill them with glue?"
And the Bishop of London said — "No."

Cheerful Charlie Chester was a comedian who by his own particular brand of wit, earnt a never-to-be-forgotten place in the minds of ordinary folk. He wrote two verses in the train, on the way to play at the Ardwick Hippodrome, Manchester —

There once was a cow in a field,
Who certainly wouldn't yield,
  The reason why
  She wouldn't try —
She disliked her 'uddersfield

A girl named 'Årdwick was struck
With a cricket ball — "out for a duck."
  Her tombstone's lonely
  With these words only —
"'Ardwick — 'ard ball — 'ard luck."

Deryck Guyler offered what must be one of the funniest offbeat limericks ever written! He told me he quoted the verse for the amusement of friends on a few occasions, and the point is that it has no rhyme!

There was a young man of Toulouse,
Who bought eleven eggs for a shilling;
His father said "Well I am surprised,"
So he went and put on his brown cardigan.

Another busy man of show business was Roy Castle. In addition to being a very good comedian, he could also sing, dance, compose, and play practically any musical instrument, including the drums. His spontaneous limericks reflected his own special brand of humour —

There was a young man writing rhyme,
Who really did not have the time.
He hurried a jot
And made a big blot
And finished up washing his shirt!

There was a young man once again
Who tried to write rhyme on a train
The train gave a lurch
And he had to search
For his pen which drove him insane!

There was an old man...
...he's still in the van!!!

Straight from the *Wireless Workshop* came a verse composed by disc jockey Kenny Everitt —

The day that the Vicar got drowned,
Just a floating dog-collar was found;
He's a watery Vicar, with a one legged knicker,
And frilly attachments all round.

Richard Murdoch had just finished playing in the pantomime *Sinbad the Sailor* at Norwich, when he found time to send these two verses.

He said he had always been intrigued by some of the place names in Norfolk — hence the following —

There was an old lady of Weasenham,
Whose bed clothes had too many fleas in 'em.
So she covered her sheeting
With masses of Keating
Which made all the fleas in 'em sneeze in 'em!

His favourite limerick was one that he first heard forty years ago — and its age is evident by the names mentioned —

There was a young lady called Gloria,
Who was "had" by Sir Gerald Du Maurier,
Jack Hilton, Jack Payne,
Then Sir Gerald again,
And the band from the Brixton Astoria.

Finally, we have Bob Monkhouse who seemed to have a flair for composing this verse form. He followed the tradition that famous people who write limericks, often have limericks written about *them*!

Here are his own special contributions, and of course he did not spare himself!

JOHN LE MESURIER

A name like Le Mesurier's curious;
Call him "*Mess-oo-rear*" and he grows furious;
Say it "*Mess-your-ee-ay*"
And he may say, "Touche!"
That's the measure of names like Mesurious.

TED RAY

"World Surrender!" screamed Mad Doctor Dread,
"Or my Thermal Eye Deathray," he said,
"Will destroy the World's Bread!"
But the corn thrived instead,
He should never have named the ray T.E.D.

LESLEY CROWTHER

Lisped a girl friend of dear Leslie Crowther's,
"I'm thick of all groanerth and groutherth;
I want thumb-one funny
To make me real thunny
And theckty ath well! Drop your troutherth!"

ERIC SYKES

Eric Sykes told the bartender, "I'm
With a girl who thinks sex is a crime;
  But when she gets tight
  She thinks it's all right —
So give me a *huge* gin and lime!"

Here is Bob Monkhouse's verse which he dedicated to himself —

"In a monast'ry," said Friar Tuck,
"Lewd brothers are pushing their luck;
  So are lecherous abbots
  With unwholesome habits —
There's a Monkhouse for that sort of muck!"

12
Postscript

Much has been written in the past few years about the literary talent that Ireland has kept hidden from the world, because of the problems of translation. I am sure that the 'lost hundred years' in the history and development of the limerick has been a factor which has contributed to the generally accepted view that its origin cannot be traced.

Also we must remember that as there were no printed books to speak of in Ireland during the era of the Maigue Poets, their limericks and other works were recorded in long hand for the amusement of the small community in which they lived. Therefore the material they wrote was never published as such, and was not circulated for the benefit of the general public.

Some historians may be of the opinion that the limerick metre was developed independently from earlier poetry patterns in this country, and that the products of the first English limerick books were not themselves influenced by the Irish limerick metre. And of course, the English versions were not named 'limericks' until towards the end of the nineteenth century.

But this does not alter the fact that the Maigue Poets of Ireland were developing and using the metrical form in the previous century. Whether the Irish metre was known to the author of *The History of Sixteen Wonderful Old Women*, is a matter for speculation.

Edward Lear popularised this verse form in the English speaking world by publishing his first *Book of Nonsense* in 1846. But still the Irish limericks as translated by Mangan were unheard of in England at that time. In fact it is only in recent years that news of the traditional Irish verses has come to light in England at all.

The Irish and English languages have not blended over the centuries. English is a mixture of many words and phrases borrowed from other tongues. French and Latin meanings for instance, are used many times. But although Ireland is in close proximity to England the Irish language has until recently remained isolated and unknown. Therefore it seems rather remarkable that the word 'limerick' should be accepted without question to describe the nonsense verse pattern made so famous by Edward Lear. Surely this fact above all others must show strongly that the form was first developed and recognised in Ireland.

A surprising number of books containing collections of limericks have been published in the last century. Many have been produced in America. Many have been printed privately to dodge censorship. Many were circulated amongst the services during the last war, to boost morale. Which ever way you look at it the limerick has not had a very hard fight for survival. Its niche in general literature may be small, but its place in the minds of ordinary folk is well established.

Many would say, and perhaps rightly so, that a book on limericks would not be complete without some 'banned' ones. Nevertheless, I am afraid that the 'blue' variety will not find a place in this publication.

To my mind unprintable limericks should remain unprinted and kept to the oral collection where they can be listened to, laughed at, and then most probably forgotten!

The Maigue Poets, and the unknown authors of the first English limericks only gloried in the new found metre, and produced unspoilt text to suit.

Lear, also, did not think to use the metre in any other way. It is later that we see how the minds of the masses gradually turned this verse form into erotic literature.

W. S. Baring-Gould's best seller, *The Lure of the Limerick*, published in Britain in 1968, contains vast quantities of limericks described as 'laundered' and 'unlaundered'. It is now in the form of a paperback, and it must be admitted that its daring contents have been the reason for its great success!

As I see it, an immoral stanza will almost automatically produce a laugh, but to compose a really funny clean one is a task only achieved by the very few. This is why competition winners score. Why, indeed, they win at all. They have produced a witty, printable, topical verse, using the restrictive metre to best advantage. A limerick poet has to have intelligence, general knowledge, and a good sense of metrical humour.

The standard of limerick making has improved over the years. Like the crossword puzzle it teases the brain and stirs the mind. It takes our thoughts off the never ending tragedies of the world, and for a while we can exercise our powers of rhyme, humour and language.

In fact it does what is very rare these days. It reminds us that we have the ability to entertain and amuse ourselves.

The British public doesn't like verse,
And Education has just made it worse;
You quote, Tennyson, Milton, Byron or Shelley,
And they shuffle their feet, and turn on the tele!
But tell them a limerick in different tone,
And soon they are busy composing their own,
Their faces are bright — they say without doubt,
"Now we can see what you're talking about!"

Jean Harrowven

BIBLIOGRAPHY

Aitken, Conrad, *A Seizure of Limericks*, W.H.Allen, 1965.

Baring-Gould, W.S., ed. *The Lure of the Limerick*, Rupert Hart-Davis, 1968.

Bishop, Morris, *Spilt Milk*, G.P.Putnam and Sons, New York, 1942.

Brock, H.I., *The Little Book of Limericks*, Duell, Sloane and Pearce, New York, 1947.

Butler, Tony, ed. *Best Irish Limericks*, Wolfe Publishing, London, 1970.

Cole, William, ed. *A Fireside Book of Humourous Poetry*, Hamish Hamilton, 1965.

Corkery, Daniel, *The Hidden Ireland*, Gill and Sons, Dublin, 1925.

de Vries, Leonard, ed. *Flowers of Delight*, Dobson, 1965.

Dineen, Patrick, *The Maigue Poets*, (Filí na Máighe), Gill and Son, Dublin, 1906.

Euwer, Anthony, *The Limatory*, James B.Pond, New York, 1917.

Godley, A.D. ed. *The Poetical Works of Thomas Moore*, London, 1910.

Green, R.L. ed. *A Century of Humourous Verse 1850-1950*, Dent, 1959.

Greene, D. and O'Connor, F., ed. and translated, *A Golden Treasury of Irish Poetry*, Macmillan, London, 1967

Holbrook, Jackson, *The Complete Nonsense of Edward Lear*, Dover Publications, New York, 1951.

Ireson, Barbara, ed. *Verse That is Fun*, Faber & Faber, 1962.

" " ed. *Poet's Corner*, Nelson, 1969.

Joyce, Mannix, 'Poets of the Maigue' article in *The Capuchin Annual*, Capuchin Publications, Dublin, 1961.

Joyce, P.W., ed. *Old Irish Folk Music and Songs*, Longmans, London; Gill and Son, Dublin, 1909.

Mac Donagh, Donagh and Robinson, Lennox, ed. *The Oxford Book of Irish Verse*, Clarendon Press, Oxford, 1958.

Milligan, Spike, *Silly Verse for Kids*, Dobson, 1969.

Nash, Ogden, *There's always another windmill*, Deutsch, 1969.

O'Donoghue, D.J., *The Life and Writings of James Clarence Mangan*, P.Geddes and Co., Edinburgh, 1871.

Reed, Herbert Langford, ed. *The Complete Limerick Book*, Jarrolds, 1925.

" " " ed. *The Indiscreet Limerick Book*, Jarrolds, 1928.

" " " ed. *Sausages and Sundials*, Jarrolds, 1927.

" " " ed. *Mr. Punch's Limerick Book*, Cobden-Sanderson, London, 1934.

Seoighe, Maichín, ed. *Glór na Máighe*, bilingual publication, Cumann na Máigre, Limerick, 1972.

Strachey, Lady, ed. *Letters of Edward Lear*, T. Fisher and Unwin, London, 1907.

Strachey, Lady, ed. *Later Letters of Edward Lear*, T. Fisher and Unwin, London, 1911.

Swann, Robert and Sidgwick, Frank, *The Making of Verse*, Sidgwick and Jackson, 1934

Thurtle, Ida, (Liza Jane), *Let's Laugh a Little*, Stockwell, Devon, 1969.

Wells, Carolyn, ed. *A Whimsey Anthology*, Dover Publications, New York, 1953.

The Dandies' Ball or *High Life in the City*, John Marshall, 1819.

The History of Sixteen Wonderful Old Women, John Harris, 1820.

Anecdotes and Adventures of Fifteen Gentleman, John Marshall, 1822

ACKNOWLEDGMENTS

Dennis Dobson, Publishers, for 'There was a Young Soldier Named Edser' and 'The Land of the Bumbley Boo' from *Silly Verse for Kids* by Spike Milligan.

Wolfe Publishing Ltd., for six limericks from *Best Irish Limericks*, ed. Tony Butler.

Andre Deutsch Ltd., London, and Little, Brown and Co., New York, for six limericks from *There's Always Another Windmill* by Ogden Nash.

Hutchinson Publishing Group Ltd., for limericks from *The Complete Limerick Book, The Indiscreet Limerick Book, Sausages and Sundials* and *Mr Punch's Limerick Book,* ed. Herbert Langford Reed.

The Estate of the Late Conrad Aitken for two limericks from *A Seizure of Limericks* by Conrad Aitkin, published by W.H. Allen.

Miss Ida Thurtle for limericks from *Let's Laugh a Little*, published by Stockwell.

The New Yorker for 'Sonnet and Limerick' by Morris Bishop © 1937, printed in *The New Yorker* in 1965.

G.P. Putnam's Sons, New York, for 'There's a tiresome young man from Bay Shore', out of *Spilt Milk* by Morris Bishop © 1942.

William Jay Smith for 'Dragon' from *A Fireside Book of Humorous Poetry*, ed. William Cole © 1957 William Jay Smith.

Dover Publications, New York, for two limericks out of *A Whimsey Anthology*, ed. Carolyn Wells.

D.C. Thompson & Co. Ltd., for limericks written by children in *Sparky* comics, issued between 1970 and 1971.

If there are any other limericks in copyright that I have used in the book and have not acknowledged, then my apologies are given.

INDEX